THE SCIENTIFIC STATUS OF PSYCHOANALYSIS

THE SCIENTIFIC STATUS OF PSYCHOANALYSIS

Evidence and Confirmation

Pushpa Misra

LONDON AND NEW YORK

First published 2016 by Karnac Books Ltd.

Published 2018 by Routledge
2 Park Square, Milton Park, Abingdon, Oxon OX14 4RN
711 Third Avenue, New York, NY 10017, USA

Routledge is an imprint of the Taylor & Francis Group, an informa business

British Library Cataloguing in Publication Data

A C.I.P. for this book is available from the British Library

ISBN-13: 9781782204060 (pbk)

Typeset by Medlar Publishing Solutions Pvt Ltd, India

Dedicated to the memory of
Professor Henry E. Kyburg, Jr
and
my brother J. Misra

CONTENTS

ACKNOWLEDGEMENTS

I thank the Indian Psychoanalytical Society for giving me permission to reprint the following article: Misra, P. (2007–2008). Scientific status of psychoanalysis: A historical account. *Samiksa, Journal of the Indian Psychoanalytical Society, 59*: 13–40.

ABOUT THE AUTHOR

Pushpa Misra is a Fulbright Fellow at the University of Pittsburgh (1993–1994) for post-doctoral research, and holds a Master's degree in psychology from Calcutta University and a doctorate in philosophy from the University of Rochester. Her academic interests range from psychoanalysis to philosophy of science, applied ethics, and literature. Her dual background in philosophy and psychoanalysis, especially her experience as a practising psychoanalyst, has given her a unique advantage to deal with the philosophical objections raised against psychoanalysis.

PREFACE

Since its inception psychoanalysis has remained the most hotly debated subject for both psychologists and philosophers. While psychologists were busy in collecting and discussing evidence for or against the various hypotheses of the theory, philosophers have concerned themselves with the more fundamental questions related to this discipline. They have concerned themselves with the logic of the theory, with the acceptability of its methodology, and, most important of all, with its status as a scientific discipline. It is the last-mentioned area that has been the topic of hottest controversy. There have been criticisms and counter-criticisms galore. Some of the major criticisms have been compiled by Sidney Hook in his book *Psychoanalysis, Scientific Method and Philosophy* (1964). Richard Wollheim's *Philosophers on Freud* (1977) also contains some major criticisms regarding the theoretical inadequacy of psychoanalysis as a scientific discipline. Every psychoanalyst worth her name is familiar with the objections levelled against the theory by Karl Popper.

In 1984, Adolf Grünbaum, the celebrated philosopher of science, published a book, *Foundations of Psychoanalysis: A Philosophical Critique* (henceforth referred to as *Foundations*). The book has been acclaimed as having said the final word regarding the scientific status of psychoanalysis.

It contains the most scathing and yet the most sophisticated criticism against the theoretical foundations of psychoanalysis as a science.

Martin Gardner on the cover page of *Foundations* hails it as a major contribution in the ever-increasing body of criticisms levelled against psychoanalysis, which he characterises as "the most persistent dogmatic establishment of recent times". The deep scholarship, the almost impenetrable logic and the clarity of the arguments that characterise Grünbaum's criticism of the claimed scientific status of psychoanalysis seem to have sealed the fate of this old controversy.

The extremely forceful language in which the arguments have been presented by Grünbaum leaves an impression of invincibility on first reading the book, which was true in my case also. However, a closer scrutiny made me revise my assessment. It became clear to me that the reasoning is not faultless though extremely sophisticated. Most philosopher-psychologists who have tried to answer Grünbaum's objections could not touch the core of his reasoning. The major fault with all the critiques of Grünbaum, in my opinion, seems to lay in their acceptance of the basic formulation of his arguments.

To cite one example, no one challenged Grünbaum's attribution of the Tally Argument to Freud; none even questioned whether the premises of the argument attributed by him to Freud are compatible with the logic of the theory. None questioned whether Grünbaum's rejection of all evidence emerging from the clinical setting is acceptable to say the least. This is true regarding almost all the responses in *Behavioral and Brain Sciences*, which published a précis of *Foundations* in its June 1986 issue with open peer commentary (henceforth referred to as *BBS Symposium*). The same may be said of the otherwise excellent book *Hypothesis and Evidence in Psychoanalysis* (1985) authored by Marshall Edelson.

In subsequent years, however, a number of articles have been published questioning the ascription of the Tally Argument to Freud. But most of these arguments were not convincing because they did not challenge the deep theoretical base in which Grünbaum's arguments are embedded. The result was that Grünbaum never gave up his initial position. In his subsequent book *Validation of the Clinical Theory of Psychoanalysis* (1993) he has essentially maintained his earlier position.

There is no doubt that a proper response to Grünbaum will require taking up the issue at a much deeper level. It requires not only a proper historical perspective (since one of the major arguments of Grünbaum is historical) regarding psychoanalysis, but also going deeper into the problems of suggestions and suggestibility. The charge that the data obtained through a clinical setting are contaminated because of the suggestions of the analyst cannot be answered unless we know with a fair degree of certainty what suggestion is capable of doing and what it cannot do. Is suggestion all powerful? Can it make a person experience an intense emotion related to some event day after day as real, even though he or she might never have experienced such an event in his or her life? If so, how long does the patient go on believing it? Does it bring about permanent change in personality or outlook towards life? These are pertinent questions related to suggestions itself. So long as we remain in the dark regarding these issues, the controversy will go on—one party attributing every success of psychoanalysis to suggestions and the other party vigorously denying it. We cannot allow suggestibility to become "Descartes' demon" as Fine and Forbes (1986) have commented, and to cast its shadow of doubt on everything.

In recent times a lot of research has been done on various kinds of suggestions and states of suggestibility. Some conclusions have clearly emerged from the medley of research that has been done in this area. A proper response to the suggestibility charge must take these findings into account. At the same time, a proper response to Grünbaum cannot depend on merely challenging his arguments. A positive and constructive approach based on the logical consequences of theory is the best way to answer charges against psychoanalysis in general and Grünbaum in particular. This is a difficult task and has been largely neglected by philosopher-psychologists. Yet such treatment of the theory alone can bring out clearly what the theory itself entails irrespective of what psychoanalysts (including Freud) and philosophers (including Grünbaum) believe that it entails.

Furthermore, no one can deny that the discussion of these problems takes us to the more general problem of whether it is reasonable to discard all the data—as Grünbaum suggests—if an uncontrollable source of error is present in the experimental situation or accept the results tentatively. What to do if an uncontrollable source of error is present in an experimental situation? Aren't there ways to deal statistically with the errors in the data? These are philosophical problems related to the general problem of confirmation of a theory. Without a thorough discussion of these aspects of the problems, no correct judgement regarding theory validation can be made in disciplines like psychology and psychoanalysis where controlling all the variables is the ideal we are continuously striving to achieve.

Yet, it has to be acknowledged that Grünbaum has pointed out some very important problems related to the scientific status of psychoanalysis. We cannot deny that more objective study of our data, more careful investigation of our causal hypotheses is required even in our clinical sessions. There is truth in psychoanalysis. But this is not sufficient. Even truth requires proof. Psychoanalysis should be thankful to Grünbaum for pointing these deficiencies out. It is hoped that more careful studies will be taken up in future by the International Psychoanalytical Association to rebut the charges levelled against it by Grünbaum and other philosophers of science.

I have tried to deal with the two most important problems that are related to the confirmation of the theory of psychoanalysis and have been raised by Grünbaum repeatedly. There are other important problems that need to be dealt with. In this connection it will not be hasty to point out that not all the fault lies with psychoanalysis. Some of the problems raised by Grünbaum are related to the tricky question of causality and causal inference. Philosophers are still struggling to come up with an acceptable theory of causality even in the area of physical and mechanical phenomena. No one would deny that the problem is more acute in the area of psychological phenomena. I shall not deal here with the very legitimate question of whether the Millian-Baconian criteria of causality can be applied to mental phenomena without modification. But let me point out that the problem lies there.

I acknowledge my deep gratitude and debt to my mentor; the late Prof. Henry Kyburg, Jr of the University of Rochester, New York. He patiently read the earlier draft of this manuscript and made meticulous and insightful comments. I have benefited enormously from these comments. In spite of his extremely busy schedule, Prof. Kyburg had always given me time whenever I wanted to discuss any points with him. I also offer my heartfelt thanks to Prof. Richard Feldman of the University of Rochester for his critical comments on the earlier draft of this manuscript. Prof. Feldman's incisive and critical comments have helped me in understanding many of the subtler aspects of the problem. He was also a great support when I despaired about the completion of the project.

In developing one of Freud's arguments, I benefited from my discussions with the late Prof. (Dr) Otto Thaler, MD, of the University of Rochester, Department of Psychiatry. In fact, I modified one of my arguments after my discussion with him. Dr Robert Goldstein, MD, of the University of Rochester, was kind enough to discuss with me some of the important problems related to hypnotic and suggestive therapies in general and gave me important references on contemporary research in these areas. I am grateful to him. My thanks are also due to Dr Leopold Bellak, MD, for sending copies of some of his works. In a friendly discussion Ms Amita Mantunga helped me in understanding some of the problems involved in the statistical testing of a hypothesis.

Last but not least, I thank Prof. Adolf Grünbaum, who was extremely kind and benevolent towards me during my stay at Pittsburgh University as a Fulbright scholar in 1994. Prof. Grünbaum allowed me to attend his seminar and sometimes helped me by supplying important references. He sent me his published articles on psychoanalysis even after I went back to India. His kind and friendly behaviour made my stay at Pittsburgh a memorable one. Dr John Erpenbeck, his wife Ilse and their lovely daughter Louisa were also a great support during my stay at Pittsburgh. Ms Sarala Kapur, a member of the Indian Psychoanalytical Society, was helpful in many ways. I offer my heartfelt thanks to all of them. I also thank the Fulbright Foundation for their support. Quite a bit of work on this manuscript was done as a Fulbright Fellow during my stay at the University of Pittsburgh in 1994. Lastly, shortcomings of the book, of which I am sure there are many, are my own responsibility.

INTRODUCTION

Writing a book to defend the scientific status of psychoanalysis is not an enviable task. While psychoanalysis as developed by Sigmund Freud has been widely practised for over a century and both practitioners and patients have proclaimed its therapeutic virtues (and some social scientists have praised its theoretical significance), there has been no dearth of critics. Some of them have doubted the efficacy of psychoanalysis as compared with that of rival therapeutic methods; others have put into question the truth of its claims, and the most radical critics have attacked it on the grounds that it allegedly fails to meet the assorted criteria of adequacy that a science ought to satisfy. It is the aim of this book to defend the theory against the criticism of the last-mentioned kind. The book is almost entirely devoted to answering the criticisms that Adolf Grünbaum has mounted against the scientific status of psychoanalysis.

In the 1960s, Karl Popper rejected the traditional inductive criterion of demarcation on the grounds that it is too weak and permissive and fails to distinguish between science and pseudoscience or metaphysics. It accords scientific status to disciplines like psychoanalysis, which, in his opinion, are metaphysical at best and pseudosciences at worst. He propounded his own criterion of falsifiability as the criterion of demarcation and concluded that psychoanalysis fails to meet his more stringent criterion and is declared outside the range of scientific disciplines.

Adolf Grünbaum seriously objected to Popper's disparagement of the inductive criterion. In a series of articles published in the seventies, Grünbaum criticised the legitimacy of Popper's criterion of falsifiability. However, for Popper the prime example of the weakness of the traditional inductive criterion was that it allows scientific status to psychoanalysis. Grünbaum takes upon himself the task of answering this objection by arguing that Popper is mistaken in claiming that psychoanalysis meets the inductive criterion. In fact, Grünbaum set out to prove a stronger claim. He set out to prove that the inductive criterion is more stringent than Popper's criterion of falsifiability. Any theory that fulfils the traditional inductive criterion automatically fulfils Popper's criterion, but not vice versa. Amid this controversy, one may wonder whether any of these philosophers were interested in finding out the truth about psychoanalysis. However, this does not totally invalidate their criticisms of psychoanalysis, though it certainly accounts for some bias in their undertakings.

Grünbaum's book *The Foundations of Psychoanalysis: A Philosophical Critique* (henceforth referred to as *Foundations*) is the most vigorous attack on psychoanalysis to date. Unlike Popper, whose criticism of psychoanalysis was perfunctory, Grünbaum has taken the trouble of familiarising himself thoroughly with the entire psychoanalytic literature. While one may disagree with Grünbaum's arguments, no one can blame him for not doing his homework. As a result, his criticisms are deeply embedded in the psychoanalytic theoretical structure and are difficult to refute. In this book I have tried to answer two major objections of Grünbaum against psychoanalysis: (i) related to the reliability of evidence that supports the psychoanalytic hypotheses, and (ii) related to the validity of the psychoanalytic arguments.

As I have mentioned earlier, Grünbaum's main objective is to show that the inductive criterion is more stringent than Popper's criterion of falsifiability. He claims that Popper's criticism of the inductive criterion is based upon a caricature of inductive criterion. Let's call a theory that fulfils Popper's criterion, P-scientific and that which fulfils the inductive criterion, I-scientific. Grünbaum is claiming that if a theory T fails to be P-scientific, it will not live up to be I-scientific, but if T is P-scientific, it does not automatically become I-scientific. The inductive criterion includes Popper's criterion of falsifiability. Grünbaum proposes to prove his claim by showing that contrary to Popper's claim psychoanalysis is P-scientific but not I-scientific.

The outline of his plan is as follows: Grünbaum first argues against the hermeneutic interpretation of psychoanalysis. According to hermeneutic interpretation, psychoanalysis does not claim to be a natural science. It is concerned with reasons, and not with causes of human actions. It deals with meanings of various actions of human beings. These meanings are deeply rooted in the history of the individual. Hence, psychoanalytic hypotheses do not make any general claim regarding the causes of human actions. In order to prove his claim, it was necessary for Grünbaum to refute this interpretation of psychoanalysis and to establish that the theoretical claims of psychoanalysis are universal claims and should be judged by the same criterion of adequacy as those of other sciences. He has argued for this thesis extensively in the Introduction of *Foundations*.

Grünbaum then proceeds to show that psychoanalysis is falsifiable, and hence it satisfies Popper's criterion of demarcation. This task he performs by listing various psychoanalytic hypotheses that have been tested experimentally, and by answering some of Popper's objections against the falsifiability of psychoanalysis. The last part of Grünbaum's argument is devoted in attempting to show that psychoanalysis miserably fails to fulfil the inductive criterion. Grünbaum claims that the major psychoanalytic hypotheses are causal in nature. The inductive criterion that Grünbaum has adopted as the criterion of adequacy for a causal claim is the traditional Millian-Baconian criterion. He uses the criterion in both its traditional version and in its more modern version in which it is used in statistical reasoning. In this connection, he points out that Mill's criterion for the justification of causal inference emphasises that the constant association of a cause C and an effect E is not sufficient to prove a causal connection between C and E. The association of C and E in absence is also required. In this requirement of negative instances we are looking for falsifying instances. Thus, Popper's criterion is included in the inductive criterion.

But while Popper's criterion would accord scientific status to a theory simply on the basis of its conceivable falsifiability, the inductive criterion requires more than mere conceivable falsifiability for a theory to be confirmed. It requires positive evidence for the credibility of a theory and the evidential credentials of psychoanalysis are, according to Grünbaum, deplorable. Its methodology is faulty, its evidence is unreliable, and the reasoning on which its arguments are based is fundamentally flawed, he says. After vigorously arguing that psychoanalysis miserably fails to fulfil the inductive criterion, Grünbaum concludes by addressing Popper again, claiming that he has shown that a theory that is I-scientific is P-scientific but not vice versa.

This book is concerned with the claims Grünbaum has made in the course of his arguments. I have not concerned myself with Grünbaum's criticism of the hermeneutic interpretation of psychoanalysis. This is because I believe that psychoanalysis did set out to establish general claims about human nature. In spite of its emphasis on the relation of neurotic symptoms with the history of the individual, its claims are clearly universal in nature. In this respect Grünbaum is right. The book is divided into two parts. Part I deals with the objections related to the unreliability of clinical evidence, and Part II deals with the objections related to the validity of psychoanalytic arguments.

The first chapter of the book serves as background. In this chapter, I briefly discuss Popper's criterion of falsifiability and his objection that the inductive criterion is too permissive. Though Popper's views about psychoanalysis are well known, I had difficulty in finding a well-formulated argument against psychoanalysis in my extensive reading of Popper. The most extensive reference to psychoanalysis by Popper is at the beginning of his *Conjectures and Refutations: The Growth of Scientific Knowledge*. So, my formulation of Popper's argument against psychoanalysis is based on the material available in this book. Very briefly, I also propose how some problems related to the introduction of ad hoc hypotheses in psychoanalysis can be handled.

Chapters Two, Three, and Four discuss Grünbaum's objections that the evidence for psychoanalytic hypotheses is unreliable and any confirmation on the bases of these data is spurious. Part II comprises Chapters Five and Six. In these two chapters, I have discussed Grünbaum's objection that the reasoning behind the repression aetiology is fundamentally flawed. Chapter Six deals with Grünbaum's more general objection that the intra-clinical setting in psychoanalysis simply lacks the resources to test the hypotheses of the theory, which inevitably leads to faulty reasoning.

Grünbaum's appraisal of psychoanalytical theory is mostly based on his reconstructions of Freud's arguments, because he thinks that in spite of the changes that the theory has undergone, the reasoning of Freud is more challenging than any other defence of psychoanalysis to date. His argument for the unreliability of psychoanalytic evidence is not an entirely new one. Essentially, it is identical with the objection Wilhelm Fliess articulated in his correspondence with Freud when psychoanalysis was still experiencing its birth pangs. This famous objection against psychoanalysis is that the analyst suggests his own ideas to the patients and the patients' responses are reflections of the analyst's suggested ideas. The evidence that is available in the clinical setting thus is highly contaminated by the suggestive influence of the analyst.

Grünbaum has given this old objection a new and sophisticated form. He has reconstructed an argument that he dubs the Tally Argument. The premises of the argument have been dubbed the Necessary Condition Thesis or NCT in short. The two premises of the Tally Argument are so called because they make the following two claims:

(1) Insight is a necessary condition for the permanent cure of a neurotic symptom.
(2) Psychoanalytic treatment is a necessary condition for obtaining insight into the causal mechanism of one's neurotic symptoms.

Grünbaum also calls it "Freud's Master Proposition". The argument has been reconstructed on the basis of the last lecture of Freud's *General Introduction to Psychoanalysis* titled "Analytic therapy". Grünbaum claims that this argument is the best defence of psychoanalysis against the suggestibility charge. If this argument is shown to be unsound, psychoanalysis is without defence against the suggestibility charge. He then proceeds to show that the Tally Argument is false. Hence, the entire epistemic status of psychoanalysis is in jeopardy. Any confirmation claimed on the bases of contaminated data is simply a spurious confirmation.

It is to be noted that the reconstruction of the Tally Argument and its demolition provides Grünbaum with the grounds to formulate his most serious objection against psychoanalysis; namely, the epistemic liability resulting from the contamination of the data. The justification for his reconstruction is largely derived from the theoretical structure of psychoanalysis. He has argued that postulation of NCT is necessary for psychoanalysis in explaining important theoretical claims. By demolishing this argument, he seeks to render the theory helpless against the suggestibility charge.

Grünbaum's reconstruction of the Tally Argument is stated in Chapter Two. In Chapter Three, I have shown that the Tally Argument neither represents the position of Freud, nor is it compatible with the logical consequences of the theory. With the help of extensive textual evidence,

I have shown that Freud could not have believed in NCT. The Tally Argument is the brain child of Grünbaum, not of Freud. It was a little disconcerting for me to note that except for Farrell no one else among the forty-five commentators on the précis of the *Foundations* published in the *Behavioural and Brain Sciences* (1986) questioned the accuracy of the attribution of the NCT to Freud. Even Farrell did not question Grünbaum's attribution of the NCT to Freud. He merely claimed that Freud did not believe in NCT for long. But Freud deserves better treatment than that. I claim that he never asserted the claims made in NCT and attributed to him by Grünbaum. As far as the logical consequences of the theory are concerned, I have not given fully fledged logical treatment to the theory. But I have formulated important hypotheses of the theory in the form of theorems and derived logical consequences from them. I have shown that the theory is not compatible with the claims that Grünbaum has ascribed to it in his NCT.

In Chapter Four, I have given an alternative reconstruction of Freud's argument based on the same lecture on which Grünbaum has based his Tally Argument. I have then discussed that in spite of its strength the argument fails to take care of the suggestibility charge in all its forms. It is to be noted that the suggestibility charge is a complex charge. Suggestions could be given in various ways and an argument that takes care of one form of the suggestibility charge may not be able to take care of other forms of the suggestibility charge. One of the difficulties in dealing with the suggestibility charge is that it is amorphous. It is not clear under what conditions even a simple instruction that is part of our everyday procedure would be considered as contaminating the data. Therefore, unless one gives the objection specific formulations the objection cannot be dealt with.

In Part II of Chapter Four, I have given my own proposal of how the suggestibility charge can be taken care of. I have argued that the suggestibility of the patient can be utilised for the purification of the data rather than being taken as an instrument for the contamination of data. I have considered the suggestibility charge as part of the general problem of error in the testing situation. I have argued that after taking proper precautions to control the major sources of error contaminating the data, we have a situation in the clinical setting that is comparable to most experimental settings. There still may be sources of error, like subtle suggestions, which cannot be completely controlled. But if we throw away the clinical data under these circumstances, we should give a similar treatment to our various experimental results, most of which contain subtle sources of error. But we do not disregard the results of our scientific investigations in spite of the fact that there are subtle sources of error present in our investigation. In fact, it seemed to me that we need some kind of theoretical justification for proceeding with our scientific activities, even though there may be possibilities of errors in our measurements. I have used Henry Kyburg Jr's theory of error to provide this justification and to argue that, in general, it is possible to test the predictions of a theory in a probabilistic way, even though all sources of error in a testing situation may not be controlled.

Part II begins with Chapter Five in which I have discussed Grünbaum's objection that the reasoning behind the repression aetiology is faulty. Grünbaum has raised two important objections to show that the inference to the repression aetiology is invalid. These two objections are related to the general problem that in arriving at repression aetiology on the basis of the cure of the patients, psychoanalysts fail to eliminate two important rival hypotheses; namely, (i) that repression could be the maintaining rather than the originating cause of the symptoms, and (ii) that the cure could be due to the placebo of suggestion.

I have argued that the distinction between a maintaining and originating cause is an artificially created one and is not justified. Regarding the elimination of the placebo of suggestion, I have argued that the concept of placebo is confusing and should be given up. Instead, the factor should be treated as a rival causal candidate, given specific formulation as a causal hypothesis and, if possible, be eliminated. I have given three specific formulations to the "placebo" hypothesis, which I call "suggestion hypothesis" and will show how they can be eliminated in a clinical setting. After answering these two objections, I have shown how a valid argument leading to repression aetiology can be formulated on the basis of clinical evidence.

Chapter Six deals with Grünbaum's general objection regarding the lack of negative evidence in the clinical setting. This, according to him, makes the clinical setting unsuitable for theory testing. I have discussed that this objection is based on misinformation; that it is possible to obtain necessary negative evidence for the retrospective testing of a hypothesis in the clinical setting by following the procedure that is typically followed in retrospective testing in epidemiology. I have also discussed Grünbaum's objections related to the faulty reasoning involved in deriving causal inferences on the basis of transference. While accepting the general legitimacy of Grünbaum's objections, I have discussed how the difficulty can be overcome.

I have concluded by discussing the experimental evidence for psychoanalysis. It was surprising for me that Grünbaum completely rejects the positive evidence of hundreds of experiments that have been performed to test psychoanalytic hypotheses. I have argued that contrary to Grünbaum's assertion, these results do provide support to psychoanalytic hypotheses. Edward Erwin, in his book *A Final Accounting: Philosophical and Empirical Issues in Freudian Psychology* (1996), has done a critical survey of the experimental results of various psychoanalytic hypotheses and in general has given a negative verdict. I have read his arguments and I hope Kyburg's theory may help in answering some of the problems related to this kind of assessment.

It is not my aim to decry the necessity of experimental evidence for the validation of psychoanalytic theory, nor do I claim that the clinical setting should be made the typical arena of theory testing. All that I am claiming is that given the peculiar nature of the theory, clinical data play an important role in the testing of psychoanalytic hypotheses, and if used cautiously they can provide us not only with valuable evidence for or against the theory, but also extremely valuable insight into the workings of the human mind; hence, Grünbaum's summary rejection of all clinical evidence seems highly unwarranted to me.

In my attempt to answer Grünbaum's objections, I have become more and more aware of the stringency of the inductive criterion he has used in judging the adequacy of the theory. I also became aware that complete chaos reigns in the area of causal inference. When we claim that being infected with the tubercle bacillus is a necessary condition for getting tuberculosis (TB) and that wherever the tubercle bacillus is absent the disease TB is also absent, we are defining TB in terms of its cause. In other words, if a patient comes with the clinical symptoms of TB and the tubercle bacillus cannot be isolated from his or her sputum, we declare that the patient is not suffering from TB. It follows from the above that a causal relation becomes analytically true and no falsifying instance could be obtained for it. In the field of epidemiology, this stringent measure for the justification of causal inference related to a microorganism was known as Koch's postulate. It required that if an organism is claimed to be the cause of a given disease, the following conditions must be fulfilled before the inference could be justified:

(1) The organism must be found in all cases of the disease in question.

(2) It must be isolated from patients and grown in pure culture.
(3) When the pure culture is inoculated into susceptible animals or man, it must reproduce the disease.

> One wonders how rigorous has been the adherence even to the first postulate. Has the tubercle bacillus been found in 100 per cent of patients with clinical manifestations of tuberculosis? No, perhaps it is found in 90 per cent of clinically diagnosed cases … A related reason for regarding the first postulate with some suspicion is that it permits a degree of circular reasoning; the clinician can decide that a disease that has all the clinical signs and symptoms of tuberculosis is not tuberculosis unless the tubercle bacillus is isolated. (Lilienfeld, 1980, p. 250)

This criterion has long been abandoned in epidemiology. Yet our intuition suggests that if C is a necessary condition for E, then C must be present whenever E is present, and E must be absent whenever C is absent. Yet we know that this association between positive and negative instances is no proof that C is causally related to E. Probably, it is a better indication than mere association in presence. But if so, there could be other indications that either alone or in combination with other factors could provide us with an equally good, if not better, indication of a causal association between C and E.

In the area of epidemiology, the causal relation is investigated in a probabilistic way mostly based on the strength, specificity and temporality of the association. The probabilistic notion of cause has its own problems. Philosophers have not been able to come up with even an acceptable definition of a probabilistic causal relation. Epidemiology justifies its methods of causal investigation by appealing to the urgency caused by a disease. They claim that causal inferences have to be derived even on insufficient evidence. The only hopeful feature is that if the investigation continues, errors involved in our causal inferences have the greater probability of being eliminated. All these problems are relevant to the choice of a criterion we employ in justifying a causal inference. However, discussion of these problems would have taken me far afield. Hence, I have discussed them in relation to their relevance regarding the problems of confirmation in psychoanalysis.

PART I

CHAPTER ONE

The background: Popper and psychoanalysis

Section I

Popper's objection against the inductive criterion

In our ordinary talk we make a kind of rough distinction between different kinds of discourses. We know that a bunch of laboratory reports is not philosophy and that a speculative discourse on the existence of God is not science. If we were asked why we think so, we would probably fumble for reasons. Philosophers of science have been trying to set up a precisely defined criterion to distinguish a scientific system from a logical or mathematical system on the one hand and from a metaphysical system on the other hand. The problem of finding such a criterion we shall call, following Popper, the problem of demarcation. The problem is not an easy one to solve and arguments and counterarguments are rampant even today.

Karl Popper, in his book *Logic of Scientific Discovery* (1959), proposed a criterion of adequacy for empirical sciences. This proposed new criterion was novel and simple. It was also revolutionary in its rejection of the verifiability criterion of demarcation—a view especially dear to the then influential logical positivist school. The logical positivist school has identified the inductive method as the characteristic method of scientific enquiries. Hence, their criterion of demarcation can be safely termed the inductive criterion of demarcation also. I shall use "verifiability criterion" and "inductive criterion" interchangeably. In order to understand Popper's argument against psychoanalysis, it is necessary to understand why he rejected the inductive criterion. After very briefly giving his reasons for this rejection, I shall explain the basic tenets of Popper's own criterion of falsifiability and his arguments against psychoanalysis.

According to the logical positivist school, a system of empirical enquiry must consist of sets of sentences that are verifiable by experience or observation. In order to be verified, an empirical statement must spell out what kind of possible observations or states of affairs will prove the sentence true. These possible states of affairs may or may not be actual. It is sufficient to specify under what conditions a statement would, in principle, be verifiable. Many logical positivists identified the meaning of a statement with the possible state of affairs for its verification. This is a semantic concept of meaning and led to the emergence of the Verifiability Theory of Meaning. It is difficult to give any precise account of this theory, but it is not needed for my purposes. It is sufficient to know that according to one formulation of the theory, the meaning of an empirical statement is identical with the conditions under which it can be verified as true.

A false statement can have as definite conditions of verification as a true one. As an example consider the following sentence: "The train is moving now". In order to understand the meaning of this sentence we have to know the possible states of affairs that, if observed, would make the sentence true. Thus, an attempt at verification of this sentence would involve finding out the truth conditions of the sentence. So, how do we go about verifying it?

> If we notice that it (the train) changes its position relative to a train on the parallel track, we are still in doubt, for it may be the latter train that really moves. But if we observe a change of position relative to station platform or relative to any object that is fixed on the earth, then we are convinced. Conclusion: The statement means semantically that the train changes the position relative to the earth. (Pap, 1962, p. 7)

Many logical positivists wanted to restrict the application of this criterion only to statements that claim to be empirical. It is obvious that a priori statements like "All bachelors are unmarried", or "If A is longer than B, and B is longer than C, then A is longer than C" do not describe any possible state of affairs that, if observed, would make them true. These statements are true or false by virtue of the meaning of terms occurring in them. Thus, to understand the meaning of these sentences it is sufficient to know the meanings of the terms occurring in them. The application of the verification criterion to a priori statements would render the distinction between empirical and a priori truths meaningless. The logical positivists, in general, did not want to do that.

Metaphysical statements are not a priori statements. At the same time, these statements do not specify any possible set of observations that, if observed, would make them true. The logical positivists considered metaphysical statements meaningless. With the help of this extremely brief description, we can state the criterion of demarcation as it was adopted by the logical positivists:

> A statement X is an empirical statement if and only if X is verifiable by a possible set of observation which will establish the truth of X. These truth conditions are identical with the meaning of X.

This strict emphasis on the observation or experience as the criterion of demarcation brought serious difficulties for the logical positivists, especially regarding the verification of scientific or natural laws. Scientific theories and laws are not always reducible to observational propositions. The long history of logical positivism is full of various attempts to reconcile the notions of scientific theories, theoretical terms, and natural laws with the notion of verification by observation statements.

However, it soon became clear that empirical statements cannot be known to be true with the degree of certainty with which "Two plus two is four" is known to be true. The falsification of even a strongly established natural law, like the law of gravitation, is not logically inconceivable. Thus, the criterion of verification of a statement was interpreted to mean the "process of finding out, coming to know that it is true" (Pap, 1962 p. 16). Each possible observation confirms the law to some degree and bestows some degree of probability that it is true. This means that the criterion of meaninglessness of empirical statements has to be expressed in terms of confirmability, rather than in terms of conclusive verifiability. We can, thus, revise the criterion in the following way:

> A statement X is an empirical statement if and only if X is confirmable by a possible set of observations which, if made, will bestow some degree of probability on X.

It is to be noted that the revised criterion does not compromise with the requirements of observations for the purposes of confirmation of an empirical statement. The reformulation merely modifies the claim regarding the degree of certainty that is bestowed on the statement under investigation. According to the positive instance theory of confirmation, evidence E confirms a hypothesis H, if E is a positive instance of H. Each instance of a black raven confirms the theory "All ravens are black".

Popper's rejection of the inductive criterion of demarcation is total. He rejects both the verifiability and confirmability criteria of demarcation. I shall begin with his argument against the verifiability criterion. The main reason why the verifiability criterion is not acceptable, according to Popper, is that it makes implicit use of inductive inference. An inference is characterised as inductive if it passes from singular or particular statements, such as statements describing the results of a number of observations, to universal statements, like hypotheses or theories. Such transitions to universal statements on the bases of singular statements, however numerous these may be, are unjustified. This problem, first raised by Hume (1740), is well known in the philosophy of science as "the problem of induction".

Popper argues that the problem of induction can be reformulated as the problem of the justification of scientific theories and laws on the basis of observation. Any claim to this must rest on an implicit use of inductive inference. As Popper says:

> Accordingly, people who say of a universal statement that we know its truth from experience usually mean that the truth of this universal statement can somehow be reduced to the truth of singular ones, and that these singular ones are known by experience to be true; which amounts to saying that the universal statement is based on inductive inference. Thus to ask whether there are natural laws known to be true appears to be only another way of asking whether inductive inferences are logically justified. (Popper, 1959, p. 28)

A point to remember in this connection is that Popper's argument depends upon his assertion that a universal statement is not logically reducible to a conjunction of particular statements. We shall, for the time being, accept this assertion.

However, in reply to Popper, it may be proposed that one way to justify inductive inferences is to establish a principle of induction, which would provide a logical basis for the transition from the singular to the universal statements. It is not clear what Popper means by a principle of induction. From his reference to Hume, it seems he refers to some principle like the principle of the uniformity of nature. If such a principle could be established successfully, it would provide a logical basis for the transition from the observed to the unobserved cases. Says Popper:

> A principle of induction would be a statement with the help of which we could put inductive inferences into a logically acceptable form. In the eyes of the upholders of inductive logic, a principle of induction is of supreme importance for scientific method: … (Popper, 1959, p. 28)

Popper argues that there are important logical difficulties in the establishment of any such principle (be it the principle of the uniformity of nature or any other principle). A principle of induction, let us call it (PI), must fulfil two requirements: (i) it must be a universal statement; (ii) it may be either an a priori or a synthetic statement.

(PI) cannot be an a priori statement because there are no such a priori principles. If there were any, the problem of induction would not have arisen in the first place. All inductive inferences would have been considered tautologically true just as all valid deductive inferences are. Therefore, (PI) must be a synthetic universal statement, a statement whose contradiction is logically possible.

If (PI) is a synthetic universal statement, we must ask the question: what justifies our acceptance of such a principle? Since it is a synthetic statement, its truth is derived from observational statement. But it is a universal statement, and we will have to formulate a principle of induction of higher order to justify such an inference on the bases of observation of particular cases. Such a process leads us to infinite regress. Popper shows that no principle of induction can be successfully established to logically warrant an inductive inference. Since the verifiability criterion is based upon the legitimacy of inductive inference, Popper concludes that the criterion too is unacceptable. Popper proceeds to argue that the reformulation of the verifiability criterion into the confirmability criterion suffers from similar difficulties and does not solve the basic problem related to the logical unjustifiability of inductive inferences. On the bases of the above objections, Popper concludes by quoting Heymans:

> "Once and for all", says Heymans, "the theory of probability is incapable of explaining inductive arguments; for precisely the same problem which lurks in the one also lurks in the other (in the empirical application of probability theory). In both cases the conclusion goes beyond what is given in the premises." (Popper, 1959, pp. 264–265)

Popper's conclusion, therefore, is that all attempts to save inductive logic and hence inductive inference from the problem first raised by Hume are destined to lead to logically unacceptable results. Hence, inductive logic must be rejected. The result of these logical difficulties for the inductive criterion of demarcation is that it fails to perform the very task for which it has been formulated. It fails to distinguish between metaphysical statements and empirical statements.

Metaphysical statements have been considered meaningless by the logical positivists because they cannot be logically reduced to elementary propositions that are testable with the help of experience. By the same logic, they have proved scientific laws meaningless also, since many scientific laws cannot be logically reduced to atomic propositions that can be verified by experiences. So, Popper concludes:

> This shows how the inductivist criterion of demarcation fails to draw a dividing line between scientific and metaphysical systems, and why it must accord them equal status; for the verdict of the positivist dogma of meaning is that both are systems of meaningless pseudo-statements. Thus instead of eradicating metaphysics from the empirical sciences, positivism leads to the invasion of metaphysics into the scientific realm. (Popper, 1959, p. 37)

Thus, with the rejection of inductive logic, Popper also rejects the inductive criterion of demarcation. With this rejection, the stage is set for Popper to propose his own criterion of demarcation.

Section II

Popper's criterion of falsifiability

Since Popper rejected inductive logic, it is clear that his own criterion of demarcation must be a deductive one. This is precisely what Popper set out to establish. He claimed that the method of science is non-inductive. Scientific theories are tested not by verification or confirmation by observation but deductively by deriving testable consequences from them.

The criterion proposed by Popper is very simple. It was clear that the distinguishing mark of an empirical discipline must be related to observation or experience in some important way. Popper pointed out that since this relation cannot be a verification of theories, it must be the falsifiability of the theories. Positive instances of white swans, however numerous, cannot justify the inference, "All swans are white". But the universal statement "All swans are white" can be falsified by a statement describing the result of a single observation of a non-white swan. The mode of this falsifying argument is modus tollens, a purely deductive argument. As Popper says:

> But I shall certainly admit a system as empirical or scientific only if it is capable of being *tested* by experience. These considerations suggest that not the *verifiability* but the *falsifiability* of a system is to be taken as the criterion of demarcation. In other words: I shall not require of a system that it shall be capable of being singled out, once and for all, in a positive sense; but I shall require that its logical form shall be such that it can be singled out, by means of empirical tests, in a negative sense: *it must be possible for an empirical scientific system to be refuted by experience.* (Popper, 1959, p. 40)

But what does it mean for a theory to be falsifiable? I shall briefly relate Popper's account of the falsifiability of a theory. In order for a scientific theory to be falsifiable, it must meet the following two requirements:

- A scientific theory must consist of sets of statements that have the logical form of an unrestricted universal conditional.
- A scientific theory must specify its basic statements. A basic statement is a singular existential statement that may serve as a premise in the empirical falsification of the theory. Such a statement must be

derivable from the theory in conjunction with the initial conditions, but not from the theory alone.

Scientific laws and theories must be expressed in a universal conditional form. Popper makes a distinction between two forms of universal statements not recognised in standard logic: (i) a strictly universal statement and (ii) a numerically universal statement. Popper explains these notions with the help of the following examples:

(i) Of all harmonic oscillators, it is true that their energy never falls below a certain amount.
(ii) Of all the human beings now living on the earth, it is true that their height never exceeds a certain amount (say 8 ft.).

The second example can be replaced by a conjunction of singular statements because it is an assertion regarding the specific elements of a finite class within a finite spatio-temporal region. The first example, however, cannot be replaced by a conjunction of singular statements unless we make the assumption that the world is bound in time and there is only a finite number of oscillators; scientific laws or theories, according to Popper, must be expressed in this logical form.

In contrast to a theory or hypothesis, which must be expressed in the logical form of a pure universal statement, a basic statement is a statement describing an observable fact within a very narrow spatio-temporal region. The latter requirement determines the logical form of a basic statement. A basic statement must be a singular existential statement. Consider the following examples:

Existential statements:	(i) There exists at least one man such that he is honest.
	(ii) There exists at least one man such that he is dishonest.
Singular statements:	(i) X (where X is an individual constant) is honest.

According to Popper, unrestricted or pure existential statements are verifiable but not falsifiable for the reason that a purely existential statement makes an assertion of the following kind: there is at least one swan that is white. It is verified as soon as a single white swan is located. But it is not falsifiable because our inability to locate a white swan does not prove that it does not exist. A purely existential statement makes a very weak assertion; hence, it is difficult to falsify. A purely universal statement makes a very strong assertion; hence it is easy to falsify.

Singular existential statements can be formed by introducing an individual constant or an individual name in a pure existential statement. For example:

> There exists at least one man in the space-time region K, such that he is dishonest.

This is obtained by introducing the individual constant "space-time region K" to the existential statement, "There exists at least one man such that he is honest". By removing the reference to the individual constant, the singular existential statement can be reduced to the form of pure existential statement.

According to Popper, a basic statement must fulfil the following requirements:

- It must be a singular existential statement;
- it must describe an observable state of affairs;
- it must be able to play the role of a test statement.

The sentences (a) and (b) below are examples of basic statements while (c) and (d) are not:

(a) There is a table lamp lighted on my table now.
(b) There is a computer on my table.
(c) If there is a raven at space-time region K, then it is black.
(d) Either there is no raven at space-time region K, or it is black.

Both sets of sentences are singular statements but the difference between them is that the former set asserts the existence of a certain state of affairs (truly or falsely); the latter does not. Since a conditional statement will be true even if its antecedent is false, it will be true even if there are no ravens at space-time region K. For this reason, positive instances of universal conditional statements cannot play the role of test statements. This brings us to the following characterisation of basic statements:

> All self-consistent singular existential statements are basic statements.

The class of basic statements is infinite. All basic statements can play the role of test statements for some theory or other. In order to play the role of a test statement for a given theory T, a basic statement must have some kind of logical relation with T. Popper admits that it is not easy to explain this logical relation. However, he proposes the following definition:

> A theory is to be called "empirical" or "falsifiable" if it divides the class of all possible basic statements unambiguously into the following two non-empty subclasses. First, the class of all those basic statements with which it is inconsistent (or which it rules out, or prohibits): we call this the class of the *potential falsifiers* of the theory; and secondly, the class of those basic statement which it does not contradict (or which it "permits"). We can put this more briefly by saying: a theory is falsifiable if the class of its potential falsifiers is not empty. (Popper, 1959)

In order to find out which basic statements are incompatible with T, we must first find out which basic statements are compatible with T. One relation of compatibility is derivability. If a statement P is derivable from a statement Q, then P and Q are compatible with each other. Therefore, if a singular existential statement S can be derived from T with the help of some other singular statements that satisfy the antecedent of T, S would be compatible with T. As we know, no singular existential statement can be derived from a pure universal statement without the help of other singular statements. Usually, these "other statements" are obtained from observation and satisfy the antecedent of the universal statement. They are known as initial conditions.

A singular existential statement S′ describing a state of affairs that, if observed, would falsify S, would be incompatible with T. S′ would be a potential falsifier of T; therefore, in order to find out whether a given theory T is empirical or falsifiable, we should first try to find out whether it is possible to derive basic statements from T with the help of initial conditions. If such basic statements can be derived from T, then determining potential falsifiers for T is a matter of logic. Any statement describing a possible state of affairs that would falsify S will be a potential falsifier for T. To illustrate with the help of an example, consider the following argument:

(T) All ravens are black.
(IC) There exists a raven at the space-time region K.
(P) There is a black raven at the space-time region K.

The statement that, if true, would falsify (P) is the following:

(P′) There is a raven at the space-time region K and it is non-black; or there is a non-black raven at the space-time region K.
(P′) is incompatible with T and is a potential falsifier of T.

We can define a potential falsifier in the following way:

> A basic statement (P′) is a potential falsifier for a theory T if and only if it is a conjunction of the initial condition of T with the negation of the derived prediction P.

We can summarise our discussion in the following way:

- A basic statement must be expressed in the form of a singular existential statement.
- No basic statement can be derived from a theory without initial conditions.
- Conditional or disjunctive statements derived as positive instances from the theory T without the help of initial conditions are not basic statements. The negation of a positive instance, however, can be a basic statement.
- If P is a basic statement, and Q is a basic statement, then "P and Q" is a basic statement provided they are consistent with each other.
- The negation of a basic statement, in general, is not a basic statement.

Falsification of a theory

The usual procedure followed in the testing of a theory T is to derive an observable prediction P with the help of initial conditions. One then tries to falsify this prediction. In other words, one tries to find out whether the potential falsifier ~P (it is not the case that P) is true or not. If ~P is found to be true, T is falsified. The mode of argument that would be applied to falsify T is simple deductive modus tollens. Let T stand for "theory" and P for "prediction", and ~P (it is not the case that P) for falsification of the prediction, then the theory is falsified by the following logical inference. If T, then P, ~P, therefore, ~T (it is not the case that T).

However, a theory is not falsified by a stray basic statement. The basic statement that falsified a given theory must be formulated in the form of a low-level hypothesis and its results must be reproducible. In other words, a theory is falsified if and only if the falsifying statement is testable, repeatable, and reproducible. It is not necessary for a falsifying effect to actually be reproduced and repeated a certain number of times. It is sufficient if it is reproducible in principle.

This is my brief account of Popper's criterion of falsifiability. We shall proceed to see how Popper has applied his criterion of falsifiability to psychoanalysis.

Popper and psychoanalysis

From our foregoing discussion, we can conclude that the falsifiability criterion of demarcation merely demands that in order to be empirical, a theory has to be falsifiable in principle. In other words, it must have a class of basic statements that, if observed to be true, would falsify the theory. The empirical status of psychoanalysis, therefore, depends on whether or not the theory has a class of falsifiers. According to Popper, the answer is negative. What are Popper's arguments to support his assertion? In fact, Popper does not seem to have a well-formulated argument. He has expressed his "opinion" in a number of scattered places. I shall quote a number of relevant portions of his opinion on psychoanalysis and try to formulate his argument on the bases of these opinions.

> ... every conceivable case could be interpreted in the light of Adler's theory, or equally that of Freud's. I may illustrate this by two very different examples of human behaviour: that of a man who pushes a child into the water with the intention of drowning it; and that of a man who sacrifices his life in an attempt to save the child. ... According to Freud the first man suffered from repression (say, of some component of his Oedipus complex), while the second man has achieved sublimation. According to Adler the first man suffered from feelings of inferiority (producing perhaps the need to prove to himself that he dared to commit some crime), and so did the second man (whose need was to prove to himself that he dared to rescue the child). (Popper, 1963, p. 35)

> But real support can be obtained only from observations undertaken as tests (by "attempted refutations"); and for this purpose *criteria of*

> *refutation* have to be laid down beforehand: it must be agreed which observable situations, if actually observed, mean that the theory is refuted. But what kind of clinical responses would refute to the satisfaction of the analyst not merely a particular analytic diagnosis but psychoanalysis itself? And have such criteria ever been discussed or agreed upon by analysts? (Popper, 1963, p. 38, footnote 3)

> Is there not, on the contrary, a whole family of analytic concepts, such as "ambivalence" (I do not suggest that there is no such thing as ambivalence), which would make it difficult, if not impossible, to agree upon such criteria? (Popper, 1963, p. 38, footnote 3)

The above are the best and severest of Popper's objections against the empirical status of psychoanalysis. At first glance, it does not seem very much. It does not even state any particular hypothesis of psychoanalytic theory and argues that the hypothesis is unfalsifiable. However, it is possible to develop Popper's objections into a cogent and strong argument. In order to fully understand Popper's point, the best thing would be to apply Popper's criterion of falsifiability to one of the psychoanalytic hypotheses and see how Popper's objection works. Let us take the following hypothesis and the prediction:

(H) All cases of hysteria are cases of repressed Oedipus complex.
(IC) P is a case of hysteria.
(Pr) P is a case of repressed Oedipus complex.

We can now derive the potential falsifier by negating (Pr):

(PF) It is not the case that P is a case of repressed Oedipus complex.
If (PF) comes out true, (H) is falsified.

Since a scientist, according to Popper, should attempt to falsify his theory rather than to confirm it, the psychoanalyst or the experimenter should try to make the potential falsifier (PF) come out true. If it does not, (H) has passed a test. But if Popper's objection against psychoanalysis is true, (H) simply cannot be put to such test. Why?

Let us consider the case of the psychoanalyst in the clinical situation who is treating P. He always finds confirmatory evidence for (H) for the following reason: the concept of Oedipus complex is so vaguely defined that any behaviour or report of P's bearing on the general topic of love for the parent of the opposite sex and anger towards the parent of the same sex will be taken as evidence of Oedipus complex. The psychoanalyst will always get confirmation of his theory too easily and the theory is never put to real test.

The more important question, however, is: could the psychoanalyst falsify his hypothesis, if he tried to? It is to be noted that this question is important to substantiate Popper's charge that psychoanalysis is not falsifiable. For, if the answer to this question is affirmative, then Popper's charge merely amounts to saying that no attempt to put psychoanalysis to the test has been made till now. Thus, the most he can claim is that the theory has not been "put to test" as per his criterion of demarcation. He will not be in a position to claim that the theory has no empirical basis, that it is not falsifiable in principle. To claim that the theory is not falsifiable in principle, Popper has to show that either:

(i) The theory lacks basic statements in the form of potential falsifiers; or
(ii) even if the formal requirement of a potential falsifier is fulfilled, the vagueness of the concepts used provides unlimited scope for the immunisation of the theory against falsification.

Under certain circumstances (ii) would amount to (i). If the crucial concepts used by a theory or by a potential falsifier are loosely or vaguely defined, it fails to provide sufficiently definite criteria for intersubjective agreement among the observers. Such a potential falsifier fails to perform its function. If the potential falsifiers of a theory are of this kind, it is equivalent to saying that the class of the potential falsifier of the theory is empty. Hence, the theory is not empirical.

We have just derived a potential falsifier for (H) above. Therefore, Popper must be understood as saying (ii). Let us see what possible arguments he can have against the testing of (PF). (PF) would be true if P does not show any sign of repressed Oedipus complex. This could be tested only if the concept of repressed Oedipus complex is defined in such a definite and precise way that the behaviour of P, his verbal report etc., is intersubjectively accepted as evidence of repressed Oedipus complex.

But the concepts of psychoanalysis are not precisely and clearly formulated. As a result, they allow the introduction of all sorts of immunisation stratagems and the introduction of ad hoc hypotheses to save the hypothesis being tested from falsification. These ad hoc hypotheses, in turn, are untestable. Hence, (PF) could never be put to the test. An example of this is as follows: let us, for the sake of argument, suppose that P does not show signs of Oedipus complex but exhibits opposite behaviour, namely hatred towards the parent of the opposite sex and love towards the parent of the same sex. Would that be accepted as the evidence for the truth of (PF) by the psychoanalysts? No, says Popper. The psychoanalyst would say that the behaviour of P is the result of reaction formation against Oedipus complex.

Can the psychoanalyst prove his contention? According to Popper, the answer is again "no". According to psychoanalysis, reaction formation is the unconsciously developed opposite tendency of the original conscious tendency. Thus, if you really hate someone, you repress it, and show love towards that person. Now, if P shows love towards the parent of the same sex and hate towards the parent of the opposite sex, a psychoanalyst would characterise it as reaction formation. Thus, a psychoanalyst could always find evidence for reaction formation and (PF) could never be found to be true.

So, the unclarity and vagueness of the crucial concepts used in psychoanalysis provide an open field for immunising stratagems for the support of the theory. By the same token psychoanalysts can explain all human behaviour by their theory and count it as confirming evidence. Every behaviour can be explained in terms of the original hypothesis or in terms of the innumerable defences that are described by the psychoanalysts. No evidence for the truth of (PF) would be acceptable to the psychoanalysts. Therefore, in principle, it is not possible to falsify the theory.

I have tried to formulate Popper's argument against psychoanalysis in a cogent way. It will be my next task to examine the validity of his objections.

Section III

Grünbaum's refutation of Popper

Grünbaum has taken upon himself the task of showing that contrary to Popper's assertion, psychoanalysis meets Popper's criterion of falsifiability, but hopelessly fails to meet the traditional inductive criterion of confirmation. In his 1979 paper "Is Freudian psychoanalytic theory pseudo-scientific by Karl Popper's criterion of demarcation?" and later in his book *Foundations*, Grünbaum argues extensively that psychoanalysis is falsifiable. I shall discuss Grünbaum's argument against Popper and try to fill some of the gaps in Grünbaum's defence of psychoanalysis against Popper.

Grünbaum's criticism of Popper's attack on psychoanalysis is twofold:

- He criticises Popper's arguments for the non-falsifiability of psychoanalysis;
- and he shows that psychoanalytic theory has testable consequences.

Michael Martin (1978) has pointed out that the consequences of a theory may be vague and/or it may not be clear what the theory implies. This leads to consequence vagueness or deductive indeterminacy affecting the testability of a theory. It is this indeterminateness of consequences that is expressed by Popper when he says that all human behaviours are explainable in terms of Freudian or Adlerian theories, thereby implying that the concepts of the theory may be stretched to fit any human behaviour.

To this Grünbaum replies as follows: if a theory T suffers from consequence vagueness or deductive indeterminateness such that it is not possible to derive testable consequences from it, then T is no more empirically supportable by inductive criterion than it is falsifiable by Popperian criterion. In this respect, the inductive criterion matches the Popperian criterion in its restrictiveness to grant scientific status to a theory on the basis of empirical evidence.

The only example of non-falsifiability that Popper comes up with is an imaginary case of two seemingly contradictory human behaviours—one of drowning a child and another of saving the life of a child—both of which, he claims, can be explained by both Freudian and Adlerian theories. But this example, Grünbaum says, cannot be accepted as a viable argument against the falsifiability of psychoanalysis for the following reasons:

(a) Popper's account is without any relevant details. He does not explicitly say how or in what way Freud's theory would explain the cases. Without these relevant details, Popper's argument is unacceptable as proof of the non-falsifiability of the theory.
(b) Popper is confusing the logical properties of the theory itself with the claim of its overenthusiastic supporters. Overenthusiastic

supporters of psychoanalysis may try to explain every case, as Popper has claimed, but this is quite independent of what the theory logically implies.

(c) Being able to explain two seemingly contradictory cases in itself is no discredit for a theory. Both cases are the types of cases that do occur in reality and a psychological theory may well be able to explain both of them too deductively. This fact, in itself, therefore, is not a discredit for the scientific status of a theory.

The objection that psychoanalysis makes unbridled use of ad hoc hypotheses is also based on wrong assumptions. There is no reason to suppose that such incidents are far greater in psychoanalysis than in physics, Grünbaum points out. Newtonian mechanics allows the use of such hypotheses if an observation result contradicts any one of its established laws. In fact, the ad hoc hypothesis of an undiscovered planet was used to explain the predictive anomaly in the course of the planet Uranus, which led to the discovery of Neptune. The hypothesis regarding the zero rest mass of neutrino falls in the same category. All these ad hoc hypotheses were introduced when no independent evidence for them was available.

It is also not true that these ad hoc hypotheses are not independently testable. For example, when an analyst introduces an ad hoc hypothesis that a given behaviour is reaction formation, he is not making an untestable assertion. The mechanism of reaction formation states that the particular defence was adopted by a given person because of the anxiety related to the original attitude. The presence of such anxiety would be a test for the hypothesis of reaction formation in a given case. Hence, the argument that unbridled use of ad hoc hypotheses makes psychoanalysis unfalsifiable is not acceptable.

What evidence can Grünbaum cite of the actual falsifiability of psychoanalysis? Grünbaum argues that if it can be shown that some of the basic and important hypotheses of psychoanalysis—both theoretical and clinical—are falsifiable in a Popperian sense, the theory may be deemed as falsifiable. Grünbaum supplies the following list:

(a) Freud's characterisation of oral and anal personality traits and their aetiological relation with specific types of psychoneurotic disorders is an eminently testable proposition. The correlation of these character traits with specific types of neurosis is also easily testable.

(b) Freud has further associated the emergence of such traits with environmental conditions like weaning and fierce toilet-training. This is also a testable proposition.
(c) In 1974, Holmes, a laboratory investigator in memory selectivity, argued elaborately that there is evidence that is adverse to the Freudian theory of repression.
(d) Freud continuously modified his aetiological hypotheses throughout his life on the basis of empirical evidence. He gave up the seduction aetiology of hysteria, his specific aetiology of obsession-compulsion neurosis, and revised his theory of dreams—all on the bases of unfavourable empirical evidence. These examples suggest that the theory is capable of being refuted by empirical evidence and that some of its hypotheses have already been refuted and modified. Therefore, it will be false to say that the theory does not have empirical content and is not testable.

Grünbaum concludes that neglecting to take these facts into account is responsible for Popper's indictment of psychoanalysis as unfalsifiable. He claims that the above examples show clearly that the theory is testable and falsifiable and meets the Popperian criterion of falsifiability.

Has Grünbaum been able to show that psychoanalysis meets Popper's criterion of falsifiability? In one sense, he has. Since psychoanalytic hypotheses are being tested—both experimentally and through statistical testing—their testability follows almost analytically. But there may be a sense in which psychoanalysis may be considered unfalsifiable. This sense is related to the following fact that psychoanalysts do not provide observational criteria for recognising a defensive behaviour as such. This lack of observational criteria gives the theory a strong weapon for the immunisation of the theory against possible falsifications. The theory does not predict any determinate observational criteria to judge a given behaviour either as the expression of the wish, or the expression of any of the defences adopted by the person. Nor is the theory able to predict whether given the initial conditions, a person would adopt a defensive attitude or not. Thus, in spite of Grünbaum's assertion that the theory is testable, one may derive the following conclusion: it is only a very small part of the theory that is directly testable. A large part of the theory is characterised by consequence vagueness and deductive indeterminateness.

This objection may have a serious consequence for Grünbaum's claim that psychoanalysis meets Popper's criterion of falsifiability. According to

Popper, a theory is tested as a whole. The hypothesis that is being tested must be related to the theory in question with a logical relation of entailment. But if it is true that only a very small part of the theory is testable, then the testable part cannot be logically related to the untestable part of the theory, because its logical relations cannot be determined clearly.

In fact, a similar objection has been raised by Frank Cioffi (1985). This objection has been strengthened by Grünbaum's assertion that the metapsychology part of psychoanalysis is untestable. Metapsychology consists of the most abstract theoretical parts of psychoanalysis. It deals with the concepts of psychic energy and different models of the structure of psychic apparatus, such as Id, ego, superego, etc., and there is sufficient reason to think that it may be untestable. At least, a large amount of refinement of concepts is needed to make this part of the theory testable. It may be objected that Grünbaum's account of the testability of psychoanalysis fails to show that the important explanatory concepts of the theory are testable. Therefore, he has failed to show that the theory is falsifiable as a whole.

Grünbaum's stand on this point is not clear. It is true that he has stated that metapsychology is untestable (Grünbaum, 1979). But it is not clear whether he takes metapsychology to be any essential part of the psychoanalytic theory. It is possible that he considers that the theory regarding the genetic development, psychodynamic propositions and aetiology of mental diseases is all that psychoanalysis consists of. Whatever it is, his stand on this point is a bit unclear.

I shall not concern myself with the psychic energy part of metapsychology. Unlike physical energy, we cannot quantify and measure psychic energy. However, therapeutic consequences based on this concept may provide it with indirect support. For example, one may predict that a neurotic person spends more and more psychic energy in maintaining counter-cathexis. Such a person will feel easily tired; will be able to accomplish little compared to a happy and normal person. Resolving the conflict, it would follow, would increase his productivity as well as the quality of his life. Similarly, if there is reason to believe that a person has a strong fixation at oedipal stage, his normal sexual relations would be hampered by it. Release of this energy would improve his sex life and would help to make it more normal. It is only in this indirect way that the theory of psychic energy could be supported.

It may of course be objected that in this formulation the theory of psychic energy is untestable. Because any cure would improve the quality of life, and this could be construed to support the theory. This, however, is not true. The theory makes the prediction that if too much psychic energy is bound to one particular kind of pleasure, some other aspect of normal libidinal gratification will be depleted. This is a testable consequence and can be tested in a broad and general way.

However, it is the problem of the introduction of the ad hoc hypotheses that probably needs further amplification in order to properly answer the objections in this area. It may be pointed out, against Grünbaum, that though ad hoc hypotheses are used in physics also, such incidents in that discipline are certainly rare. In psychoanalysis the main complaint against its testability is the unbridled use of such immunisation techniques. A more elaborate defence of this aspect is needed.

Though this charge of unbridled use of ad hoc hypotheses has been voiced again and again, a person familiar with the theory may wonder how justified this accusation is. Psychoanalytic theory characterises specific defences in very determinate and specific ways. Defence mechanisms do not cover the whole range of normal behaviour of human beings. It would be false to say that all conceivable human behaviour could be explained by introducing ad hoc hypotheses about defences. This is not to deny that some psychoanalysts might try to do so, or, as Grünbaum has pointed out, overenthusiastic supporters of the theory may try to explain all conceivable human behaviour by manipulating the theory to fit the data. But this is different from what the theory implies.

The reason that the so-called immunisation techniques of psychoanalysis have provoked such strong objection against the testing of psychoanalysis is twofold:

- The difference between a defensive behaviour and a normal behaviour is not apparent to an ordinary observer;
- psychoanalysis has not been able to provide definite initial conditions for predicting the adoption of particular defences by a particular individual or types of individual.

However, so far as an analyst is concerned, he clearly observes the defensive behaviour. Usually an expert analyst is able to discern between a defensive behaviour and a normal behaviour. The analyst is a trained observer and can perceive many small and subtle signs that escape the eyes of an untrained observer. The analyst often observes a personality as generally defensive by observing the rigidity in the movement of the person, in the manner of his or her speech and in other behavioural manifestations. But this expert observation does not constitute evidence for the testing of a theory. And, maybe, it is this expert observation that is being put to the test. Is the expert observer's observation merely a subjective fantasy to provide spurious confirmation to his theory or is there some objectivity in this observation?

If the theory could provide exact initial conditions that would help in predicting a given defensive behaviour, the problem of ad hoc immunisation of the theory could easily be solved. Unfortunately, psychoanalysis cannot yet provide such exact initial conditions. There are, however, fairly definite ways in which a defensive behaviour can be singled out from normal behaviour. In this connection, I shall discuss only the general schema that would help in testing or finding independent evidence for a particular type of defence mechanism.

We need the following kind of evidence in order to test whether the introduction of ad hoc hypotheses is justified or not:

(a) Evidence that such defensive behaviours exist.
(b) Specified conditions under which people tend to adopt such defences.
(c) Characteristic features of a defensive behaviour that would distinguish it from normal behaviour.

This is a difficult demand to fulfil. However, some progress has been made to test whether the so-called defences exist or not. Hilgard, Kubie and Pumpian-Mindlin (2012) and Erdelyi (1985) report a number of studies that confirm the existence of such defence mechanisms as repression, projection, displacement of aggression, and regression. I shall, therefore, proceed on the assumption that such defensive behaviours exist or their existence can be tested under laboratory conditions.

In a test situation, we are more concerned with (b) and (c). In fact, (b) and (c) could test (a) also. Let us suppose a given behaviour has been characterised as reaction formation. How can we test whether it is so? There are two possible ways of testing:

(i) By finding out whether the behaviour has the characteristic features of the said defensive behaviour (c); and
(ii) by trying to find the existence of the hypothesised psychodynamic factor that necessitated the adoption of the specific defence mechanism in the first place.

The characteristic features of a defensive behaviour have been clearly described in the case of reaction formation. A behaviour that is characterised by excessive rigidity is usually considered to be reactive in origin. The question then arises as to how to determine the degree of normal rigidity or excessive rigidity of a cluster of human behaviours. This is not an unsolvable problem. A group of clinicians (they may or may not be psychoanalytically oriented) can be employed to rate the subjects in terms of rigidity related to specific behaviours that have been designated as being reactive in origin. In fact, such studies have already been done (see, Fischer & Greenberg, 1978). If inter-judge rating pronounces the behaviour of the person within the acceptable range, the hypothesis should be considered falsified.

Finding the existence of the hypothesised psychodynamic factor is more difficult to assess and requires more sophisticated testing. The hypothesis of reaction formation specifies some psychodynamic initial conditions under which such behavioural defences have been adopted. Experiments have to be designed to test whether such initial psychodynamic factors are present in the case of the subjects under investigation. For example, the reactive kindness and politeness of a person is hypothesised as having originated from aggressive tendencies that a person has difficulty in managing and which causes him or her anxiety. One way of testing the hypothesis of reaction formation is to design an experiment to tap into this unconscious hostility. More specifically, if expression of aggression is associated with strong anxiety (a suggestion made by Grünbaum), this would also support the hypothesis of reaction formation.

Quite a few tests have been designed to tap into such dynamic factors to test the theory of defence mechanisms as well as some aetiological hypotheses of psychoanalysis. Projective tests can be successfully used to demarcate the area of conflict; in this particular case, aggression.

Another way of providing evidential support for ad hoc hypotheses is to predict further behavioural characteristics of the person. For example, the psychoanalyst can more or less confidently predict that subjects whose cleanliness is reaction formation against the original opposite tendency would display in greater proportion the cluster of anal-type personality traits. In addition to these, subjects can be tested with regards to their ability to manage money and time, which is related to anal cluster traits. Thus, the general schema for the testing of the ad hoc hypotheses related to a defence mechanism would involve the following:

(a) An expert opinion that a given behaviour B is defensive.
(b) An expert opinion as to whether there are distinguishing features of B that could distinguish it from normal behaviour of the same kind.
(c) If B is characterised by some kind of excessiveness, employ inter-judge rating to test the claim.
(d) Test the presence of the psychodynamic factor F theorised to be causally connected with the adoption of B in the first place.
(e) In therapy, if the removal of F leads to a change in the nature of B, or is accompanied with discernable modification in B, it should prove that the ad hoc hypothesis was not ad hoc after all. In doing so, there should be evidence that change in F is causally related to change in B.

By adopting (a) to (e) one can test many hypotheses related to major defence mechanisms. Ad hoc hypotheses related to defence mechanisms are not untestable, though designing experiments to test them requires ingenuity as it does to test all psychoanalytic propositions. Similarly, deductive indeterminateness of the theory of psychoanalysis is no longer considered a big hurdle in testing these hypotheses. Usually, the crucial concepts used in an experimental testing are given a sharp definition in the context of a given enquiry. Disagreement about such a definition is not rare, but the process keeps on moving with the help of corrections and counter-corrections. Hence, there may have been some truth in Popper's claim at the time he made it. But more and more laboratory experiments are being devised to test psychoanalytic hypotheses, proving that the difficulty is not insurmountable.

In next chapter, I shall discuss Grünbaum's claim that contrary to Popper's assertion, psychoanalysis fails to meet the inductive criterion of confirmation.

CHAPTER TWO

The inductive criterion

Section I

The necessary and sufficient condition

I shall now proceed to discuss Grünbaum's argument that psychoanalysis fails to meet the inductive criterion of demarcation. Grünbaum has accepted the inductive criterion of confirmation as I have described it in the previous chapter. Since most of the psychoanalytic hypotheses are universal causal hypotheses, this criterion of confirmation has to be supplemented by the special conditions required for the confirmation of causal hypotheses. Grünbaum says:

> For brevity I shall say of a theory T that "T is I-scientific" iff it qualifies as *inductively* scientific or *well*-supported by the neo-Baconian standards of controlled inquiry: For our purposes, the attribution of inductive well-supportedness to T by all the available pertinent evidence E does *not* require that E render T more likely to be true than false, but this attribution requires that E confer *greater credibility* to T than any of its available rivals. (Grünbaum, 1979)

The modern version of Mill's method referred to in the above passage is the reformulation of Mill's criterion in terms of necessary and sufficient conditions by Von Wright and its application in the testing of causal hypotheses. This criterion can be used (i) either as a predictive-explanatory model as is done in hypothetico-deductive method or (ii) as a stochastic model as is done in the statistical testing of causal hypotheses. In any case, the evidence will support the hypothesis only in a probabilistic way. Psychoanalytic hypotheses, Grünbaum claims, fail to meet both (i) and (ii).

Before I start discussing Grünbaum's objection against psychoanalysis, a few points related to the justification of a causal hypothesis need to be mentioned. Mill's criterion is well known and does not require any elaborate discussion. The notion of causal relevance advocated by Mill was that of constant or invariable association of two properties or groups of properties. Modern statistical hypotheses use a probabilistic notion of causal relevance. A causal hypothesis makes an assertion of the following kind: A relation R of causal relevance exists between two properties X and Y. Grünbaum considers the notion of causal relevance in the following three senses:

(i) X is causally necessary for Y.
(ii) X is causally sufficient for Y.
(iii) X is stochastically (probabilistically) rather than invariably a cause of Y.

This is neither a mutually exclusive nor an exhaustive list of causal relevance but merely states the three important characterisations of causal relevance. In a causal investigation, the property whose necessary or sufficient condition is being investigated is called the conditioned property and the properties that are possible candidates for the necessary or sufficient conditions for a given conditioned property are known as the possible conditioning properties. "Sufficient conditions" and "necessary conditions" are defined in the following way:

- X is a sufficient condition for Y if and only if whenever X is present Y is present.
- X is a necessary condition for Y if and only if whenever Y is present X is present.

It is difficult to provide an uncontroversial definition for the probabilistic notion of causal relevance. It is better to accept the notion applied in the statistical testing of causal hypotheses, which may be described in the following way:

> X is stochastically causally relevant to Y if and only if P (Y/X) is greater than the P(Y). (Read, probability of Y given X is greater than the probability of Y.)

The above definition takes into account only positive causal relations between two properties X and Y. Statistically, X is causally relevant to Y in a negative way also, that is, X is causally relevant to Y if the P(Y/X) < P(Y). (Read, the probability of Y given X is less than or equal to the probability of Y.)

The definitions above are to be read with a "ceteris Paribus" clause. The reason for this is that when we make an assertion of causal relevance in either of the senses given above, we assume a whole lot of conditions that are too obvious to mention. For example, when we say that putting the sugar in water is sufficient to dissolve it, we assume that the water is not already saturated; its temperature is of the right kind, etc. Thus, our assertion of causal sufficiency takes the following form:

> To say that X is a sufficient condition for Y is to assert that X was followed by Y or will be followed by Y, and the conditions under which X occurred—call them Z—are such that an event similar to X in the presence of Z will be followed by an event similar to Y.

In asserting that X is a sufficient condition for Y, we are also asserting that if Y fails to occur in the presence of X, then X is not a sufficient condition for Y. This denial of the relation of sufficiency should not be taken as an unconditional denial. Thus, to say that turning the TV switch on is a sufficient condition for getting a TV programme on the TV screen is to say that an event like turning the TV switch on will be followed by an event like the reflection of pictures on the TV screen, given the conditions Z, which in this case are the TV not being out of order and programmes being broadcast from TV channels, etc. This account makes us think that what we call the sufficient conditions are really not sufficient conditions. These conditions are all individually necessary and are sufficient only in conjunction with some other assumed conditions Z.

Second, do we then mean, in the sense given above, that our search for causal relevance is a search for necessary conditions only? In the strictest sense, this is false. In our search of necessary conditions also, we assume a whole set of conditions without mentioning them. To say that the pressing of the gas pedal is a necessary condition for starting the car is strictly to say that no incidence of car-starting will take place without a preceding incident of pressing the gas pedal. At the same time, it seems reasonable to say that pressing the gas pedal is a necessary condition to get the car started even though there are cases where a car has started without the gas pedal being pressed. What is truly meant is that pressing the gas pedal is a necessary condition for getting the car started, provided that nobody is pushing the car from behind, or that the car is not on an incline, etc. (Pap, 1962, pp. 254–255).

In other words, an event A is a necessary condition for another event B given certain other necessary conditions C. Thus Grünbaum defines universal causal hypothesis in the following way: A hypothesis H is a universal causal hypothesis if and only if H makes a non-tautological assertion that logically implies that either X is causally necessary for Y or X is causally sufficient for Y, ceteris paribus (see Grünbaum, 1977). A positive instance of a causal claim can be defined regardless of the type of causal relevance asserted in a causal hypothesis. A positive instance (I) of a universal causal hypothesis (H) would be an instance of the hypothesised cause X, which is also an instance of the hypothesised effect Y.

Mill's methods are known as the methods of eliminative induction. The sufficient and necessary conditions are discovered by eliminating rival candidates one by one, by applying the definitions of necessary and sufficient conditions mentioned above. When we are looking for a sufficient condition, we try to look for conditioning properties (the supposed causal properties) that are absent when the conditioned property (the effect) is absent. A property P cannot be a sufficient condition for a conditioned property E if P is present when E is absent.

When we are looking for necessary conditions, we try to find out if the conditioning property (the causal factor) is always present when the conditioned property (the effect) is present. A conditioning property P cannot be a necessary condition for a conditioned property E, if P is absent when E is present. We can formulate the rules of elimination in the following way:

(a) X is eliminated as a sufficient condition for Y, if X is present and Y is absent.
(b) X is eliminated as a necessary condition for Y, if Y is present and X is absent.

These rules of elimination are also the rules of justification of a causal inference. Suppose a physician claims that vitamin C is a necessary condition for curing the common cold. He has evidence that whenever vitamin C is given to patients suffering from a common cold they are cured or are cured faster than usual. This meets our positive criterion that a necessary conditioning property must be present whenever the conditioned property E is present. But this list of positive evidence is insufficient to establish a relation of necessity between vitamin C and the common cold, because the correlation may be merely accidental. To test this, the physician has to collect negative instances as well. He has to observe instances of people suffering from a common cold and not being given vitamin C. If a single instance of cure is observed in this group (all other things being the same) then as per our rule (b), vitamin C is eliminated as a necessary condition for the cure of a common cold. Cure was present when vitamin C was absent. Hence, it cannot be a necessary condition for cure.

Similarly, to test whether a possible conditioning property P is a sufficient condition of a given conditioned property E, it is not sufficient to show that P was absent when E was absent. This agreement in absence again may be coincidental. One has to look for instances where P was present but E was absent. If such a case is found, P is eliminated as a sufficient condition for E according to our rule (a). Thus, according to the example given above, if our physician claims that vitamin C is a sufficient condition for curing a common cold, it is insufficient evidence if he has merely the evidence that vitamin C was the only conditioning property that was absent when the cure from the common cold was absent. The physician also has to observe test cases where vitamin C was given but the cure was absent. If such a case is observed, the causal inference that vitamin C is a sufficient condition for cure of the common cold is unjustified.

Usually one may arrive at a tentative causal conclusion by using Mill's single method of agreement, but to test the conclusion thus arrived at, Mill's joint method of agreement and difference and joint method of agreement are used. Both these methods are the most widely used methods in social sciences for testing tentative causal discoveries. Practically in all circumstances, the use of the double method of agreement is recommended to test the conclusions arrived at by the single method of direct agreement. It is the double method of agreement that is used in the form of control group and experimental group procedures widely used in epidemiology and other social sciences. As Arthur Pap points out:

> If the scientist who compares an experimental group with a control group aims at the discovery of a necessary condition, then the double method of agreement is appropriate. For if the members of the experimental group agree in no relevant respect except the tested factor, and the members of the control group agree in the absence of the tested factor and in the absence of the effect, then the hypothesis that the tested factor is a necessary condition for the effect has been confirmed. On the other hand, experimental and control group may also be compared in conformity to the requirements of the method of difference, which is appropriate for eliminating possible sufficient conditions. In that case care is taken to make the two groups as similar as possible in relevant respects, so that they differ relevantly only with respect to the tested factor. (Pap, 1962, pp. 153–154)

It is important to take note of this requirement of negative instances for the justification of a causal inference. Whether the hypothesis being tested is a universal hypothesis as defined earlier or a non-universal hypothesis as in statistical confirmation of causal hypotheses, without the supporting evidence of such negative instances no causal inference is justified.

It is to be noted, however, that even in the case of a statistical hypothesis the evidential support of the causal hypothesis is not provided by the number of positive instances in a group however large that number may be. The evidential support has to come from a comparative estimate between the experimental and control group. The occurrence of the effect in the experimental group must exceed a required quantity or quality in comparison to the occurrence of the said effect in the control group. Thus, in case of a universal causal hypothesis (H), a negative instance may refute the hypothesis, but in case of a non-universal or statistical hypothesis (H′) the negative evidence may disconfirm (H′) though it will not falsify (H′).

This essential requirement of negative instances for the justification of a causal hypothesis implies that the inductive criterion includes Popper's criterion of falsifiability. As Grünbaum says:

> … only the combination of positive instances with instances of non-X and non-Y could constitute inductively supportive instances

> of our strong causal hypothesis H. And obviously the logical possibility of such supportive instances goes hand in hand with the logical possibility of refuting instances! Thus, cases of X and non-Y or non-X and Y would each be refuting instances for H, if we may presume that the *ceteris paribus* proviso is fulfilled in the first set of these. Moreover, *if* we are able to identify supportive instances observationally, we can likewise empirically identify falsifying instances. (Grünbaum, 1977)

Thus, according to Grünbaum, if a hypothesis (H) has fulfilled the criterion of being I-scientific, it has automatically fulfilled the criterion of being P-scientific.

This brief survey of necessary and sufficient condition is sufficient for our purposes. The account of cause as a necessary or sufficient condition is related to our interest in causality. If we want to produce an effect, we would like to bring about the sufficient condition, and if we want to prevent an effect from occurring, we would like to prevent the presence of a necessary condition. As Brian Skyrms says:

> Remember, however, that everything that has been said about Mill's methods, and everything that can be said about their more involved forms, rests on two simple principles of elimination:
> i. A necessary condition for E cannot be absent when E is present;
> ii. A sufficient condition for E cannot be present when E is absent. (Skyrms, 1966, p. 105)

Before we take up Grünbaum's objections against psychoanalysis, it is only fair to mention that not all causal hypotheses can be tested by forming control and experimental groups. Hypotheses in astronomy, meteorology and other such sciences deal with phenomena that cannot be brought within the range of experimentation. The method of testing such causal hypotheses is the hypothetico-deductive method, which we have discussed in the previous chapter. A successful prediction derived from the hypothesis being tested with the help of the initial conditions provides confirmation of the hypothesis. However, two important points have to be taken into account in this connection.

First, the improbability of the success of a prediction is a relevant factor in conferring confirmation to the hypothesis being tested. The more improbable the success of a prediction, the greater is the degree of confirmation. Second, since the hypothetico-deductive model is an explanatory model also, a hypothesis may claim confirmation on the basis of its explanatory power. A statement S describing a state of affairs may be explained by a theory T by showing that S logically follows from T. In this context, the inductive criterion imposes a restriction that Grünbaum calls the declared consequence restriction. This restriction may be described as follows:

> … *the construal of T at any given stage of its development* be such as to allow the fulfillment of the following requirement by any empirical statement S which is compatible with T: If, at a particular time, S is *declared* to be a logical consequence of T under the assumption of stated initial conditions, or is declared not to be such a consequence, then *neither* declaration is allowed to depend on knowing at the time whether S is true. (Grünbaum, 1979)

Put simply, the deductive derivability of a statement S from a theory T does not confer any confirmatory status on T if S is already known to be true at the time of deduction.

Suppose, T claims: exposure to X-radiation beyond a certain degree causes cancer. Given the initial condition that P has been exposed to X-radiation beyond the degree specified in T, the predictive statement S will be: there is a high probability that P will suffer from cancer. But if P already suffers from cancer at the time S was derived from T and the fact was known to be so, then S fails to bestow any confirmation on T. In order to test a theory with the help of the hypothetico-deductive method, the theory has to be put to risk. If the statement predicted is already true at the time of prediction, it does not put the theory at risk of falsification and hence does not genuinely test the theory.

One may wonder whether this declared consequence restriction is too strong. Einstein's theory explained the slight discrepancy in the course of Mercury that could not be explained by Newtonian theory. This was counted as providing evidential support to Einstein's theory, yet the discrepancy in Mercury's course was known to be true at the time it was explained by Einstein's theory. All that is required in such contexts is that S not play any role in the structure of the theory.

With this brief introduction about the inductive criterion of justification adopted by Grünbaum, we are now ready to state his objection that psychoanalysis fails to meet this criterion.

Section II

Grünbaum's charge against psychoanalysis

Grünbaum's attack on psychoanalysis is both extensive and intensive. He has subjected the basic tenets of psychoanalysis to scathing criticism in his attempts to show that Popper's charge against the inductive criterion is false; that the inductive criterion does not provide any confirmatory status to psychoanalysis. He aims to achieve his objective by showing that:

(a) The claimed confirmation of the psychoanalytic theory is spurious. The major claim of confirmation of psychoanalytic hypotheses is based on clinical evidence. This evidence is unreliable and contaminated by various sources of error. The chief source of error is the suggestive influence of the analyst on the analysand. Let us call this charge, the suggestibility charge.

(b) Even if one grants that the clinical data are uncontaminated, the arguments supporting the major hypotheses of the theory are invalid. In particular, the arguments supporting the following basic hypotheses of psychoanalysis are invalid:
    (i) Repression is the cause of psychoneurotic disorders.
    (ii) Repressed conflict is the cause of parapraxes.
    (iii) Infantile repressed wishes are the causes of dreams.

Grünbaum has elaborately argued the above points in his book *Foundations* and the precis of *Foundations* published in *Behavioral and Brain Sciences* (henceforth referred to as *BBS Symposium*). He has concluded:

> The inductivist methodology I used to assess Freud's causal hypotheses is the modern version of the centuries old tradition going back to F. Bacon and J. S. Mill. On this basis Chapters 1–10 reached a rather negative conclusion about the clinical evidence for the theory of repression, and *even about clinical testability in general*. As is now clear, the clinical validation of psychoanalysis would be

> no more acceptable to a traditional inductivist (like Bacon or Mill) than to Popper ... Hence, the specifically clinical support claimed by many Freudians, but rejected by inductivism, can no longer be used as a basis for Popper's charge that an inductivist criterion of demarcation between science and nonscience is too permissive. (my emphasis) (*BBS Symposium*, p. 228)

Grünbaum's dual attack on the soundness and validity of psychoanalytic arguments, if successful, will seriously affect the epistemological status of psychoanalytic hypotheses. I propose to defend psychoanalysis against the specific charges of Grünbaum mentioned above. I shall first present Grünbaum's argument related to the unreliability of clinical evidence. My reply to this objection against psychoanalysis will involve the following two steps:

(1) I shall show that Grünbaum's argument against the unreliability of clinical data is untenable and highly exaggerated.
(2) I shall discuss the general problem of error in relation to the clinical validation of psychoanalytic hypotheses and argue for the intra-clinical testing of psychoanalytic hypotheses under specified conditions.

After discussing the problems related with the reliability of clinical evidence, I shall discuss Grünbaum's objections related to the invalidity of the arguments leading to major psychoanalytic hypotheses. In this connection, I shall limit my discussion only to the defence of repression aetiology:

(i) I shall show that it is possible to formulate a valid argument for repression aetiology.
(ii) I shall discuss a number of important problems related to the validity of causal inference in psychoanalytic case studies and discuss how they can be overcome.

I begin by presenting Grünbaum's argument for the suggestibility charge against psychoanalysis. It is important to realise that the objection I am presenting below is perhaps Grünbaum's most important objection against psychoanalysis. The argument that

Grünbaum has developed is deeply embedded into the structure of psychoanalytic theory.

Grünbaum's argument against the reliability of clinical evidence is based upon the suggestive influence of the analyst on the analysand during the course of therapy. He points out that the psychoanalytical method of treatment essentially consists in bringing about the repressed unconscious memories and experiences of the analysand to the conscious mind and helping him or her to adjust to them without further repression. In the course of treatment, the analysand inevitably undergoes a process of "transference" towards the analyst. Depending upon the positive or the negative feelings experienced by the analysand towards the analyst, the transference is called either positive or negative. During the state of positive transference, the analysand is favourably disposed towards the analyst and is in a highly suggestible state of mind towards him. The analyst exploits this influence on the analysand by directing him or her to bring up the materials (repressed memories and experiences) that are supposedly the cause of the malady the analysand is suffering from. Major therapeutic work in psychoanalysis is done during this state of transference of the patient.

The suggestibility charge against psychoanalysis runs as follows: the repressed memories and other materials that are supposedly the cause of the neurotic symptoms are brought about by the analysand under the suggestive influence of the analyst. The same data are used as confirmatory evidence for the psychoanalytical hypotheses. Under these circumstances, the veridical nature of the data becomes highly suspect. The data might have been produced by the analysand under the indirect influence of the analyst in order to please him. Thus, the alleged confirmation of the psychoanalytical hypotheses on the bases of these data is highly suspect. Since there is a possibility of the epistemic contamination of the clinical data, any claim of confirmation based upon these data is highly unreliable.

There are two ways to counter the suggestibility charge:

- By empirically determining whether the data are contaminated by the suggestive influence of the analyst in such a way that they provide a self-validation of the theoretical hypotheses.
- By logically showing that at least the data regarded as evidence for a hypothesis under investigation are highly unlikely to be contaminated.

There are obvious difficulties in adopting the first course. Chief among these is our ignorance of ways and manners in which indirect suggestion may influence the thoughts, feelings, memories and other psychological states of the person being analysed. Also, this policy will provide validation only in individual cases where such investigation has been carried out. It will fail to answer the suggestibility charge in general. So, a number of attempts have been made to counter the suggestibility charge by adopting the second approach.

In his twenty-eighth lecture "Analytic therapy" in *Introductory Lectures on Psychoanalysis* (1916–1917), Freud takes upon himself the task of answering this charge. On the basis of this lecture, Grünbaum has constructed an argument that, he thinks, is the best defence against the suggestibility charge he has encountered in psychoanalytic literature. He argues that Freud's argument is unsound. If this argument fails, Grünbaum claims, there is no defence that can save psychoanalysis from the enormous epistemic liability it faces due to the possible contamination of its data.

In his lecture "Analytic therapy", Freud squarely addresses the suggestibility issue first by stating that in psychoanalytical therapy the analyst uses suggestion in an educative sense to help the analysand overcome his or her resistance and to bring up the materials that are causally related with his or her symptom. Freud then proceeds to enunciate the difference between suggestion used in purely suggestive therapy like hypnosis, and suggestion used in psychoanalytical therapy. Finally, Freud gives his reasons why the therapeutic results obtained in psychoanalysis could not be due to suggestion. Since this passage is the basis of Grünbaum's reconstruction of Freud's argument, I shall quote it at length:

> But you will now tell me that, no matter whether we call the motive force of our analysis transference or suggestion, there is a risk that the influencing of our patient may make the objective certainty of our findings doubtful. What is advantageous to our therapy is damaging to our researches. This is the objection that is most often raised against psychoanalysis, and it must be admitted that though it is groundless, it cannot be rejected as unreasonable. If it were justified, psychoanalysis would be nothing more than a particularly well-disguised and particularly effective form of suggestive treatment and we should have to attach little weight to all

> that it tells us about what influences our lives, the dynamics of the mind or the unconscious. That is what our opponents believe; and in especial they think that we have "talked" the patients into everything relating to the importance of sexual experiences—or even into those experiences themselves—after such notions have grown up in our depraved imagination. These accusations are contradicted more easily by an appeal to experience than by the help of theory. Anyone who has himself carried out psycho-analyses will have been able to convince himself on countless occasions that it is impossible to make suggestions to a patient in that way. The doctor has no difficulty, of course, in making him a supporter of some particular theory and in thus making him share some possible error of his own. In this respect the patient is behaving like anyone else—like a pupil—but this only affects his intelligence, not his illness. After all, his conflicts will only be successfully solved and his resistances overcome if the anticipatory ideas he is given tally with what is real in him. Whatever in the doctor's conjectures is inaccurate drops out in the course of the analysis; it has to be withdrawn and replaced by something more correct. (Freud, 1916–1917)

On the basis of this passage, Grünbaum has reconstructed Freud's argument, which he calls the Tally Argument.

The Tally Argument

The Tally Argument is constructed as follows:

(Pr.1) The psychoanalytic method of interpretation, etc. is necessary to gain insight into the unconscious causal mechanisms of one's neurotic symptoms.
(Pr.2) This insight is a necessary condition for the cure of P's neurotic symptoms.

Grünbaum dubs these two assumptions The Necessary Condition Thesis of Freud or in short NCT. He also calls it Freud's Master proposition. A bit of explanation regarding the use of the word "insight" seems to be in order here. In psychoanalysis the word "insight" has been used in relation to the understanding of a causal mechanism, often involving unconscious motivations, wishes, desires, etc., which are responsible for giving rise to a problem behaviour or attitude.

To give a very simplified example, suppose P is having continuous problems with his wife. P is said to have "insight" when, in the course of therapy, he comes to realise that the kind of behaviour he is seeking from his wife is predominantly that which he received from his mother. He was, however, not aware of what was making him unhappy about the behaviour of his wife. This "insight" is to be accompanied by appropriate emotional experiences. Insight is not always dependent on giving a gapless "causal account" of a problem behaviour or attitude. That would be a circular account of insight or cause.

Can there be a "pseudo insight"? The word is being used in current literature to designate "a false understanding of the causal mechanism". It is to be noted, however, that a "pseudo insight" is a false understanding, not a true one. Insight by definition would be true.

Now to come back to Grünbaum's argument: Grünbaum claims that given the existence of such successfully treated patients P, and NCT, Freud derived two conclusions about "any and all patients P who emerged cured from their analyses" (*Foundations*, p. 140):

(1) The psychoanalytic interpretations of the hidden causes of P's behaviour given to him or her by the analyst are indeed correct, and thus—as Freud put it—these interpretations "tally with what is real" in P.
(2) Only analytic treatment could have wrought the conquest of P's psychoneurosis.

Because of the use of the catching phrase "tally with what is real", Grünbaum calls this argument the Tally Argument. On the basis of the Tally Argument, Grünbaum says, Freud proceeds to justify the following epistemological claims:

- The durable therapeutic success of psychoanalytic treatment guarantees that the interpretations given to the analysand are indeed veridical or at least quite close to the mark.
- The collective success of psychoanalytic therapy is cogent evidence that the specific aetiology of psychoneurosis, as well as the general theory of personality given by Freud, is indeed correct.

- The psychoanalytic method of probing the unconscious is also vindicated as a method of aetiologic investigation.
- The method validates the major causal claims of the theory without the burden of conducting any prospective longitudinal enquiries.

If NCT is true, Freud can indeed claim the above. The success of psychoanalytic therapy will vindicate the truth of its theory. Given the first conjunct of NCT; namely, that the psychoanalytic method of treatment alone can provide P insight into the causal mechanism of his symptoms and supplemented by the second conjunct that insight alone can lead to a durable cure; the stage is set for the confirmation of the theoretical hypotheses of psychoanalysis through the success of its therapy. If P is cured of his neurotic symptom S, it would follow that he had undergone psychoanalysis and had insight. He could not have insight if the interpretations of his analyst were false. So, the interpretations must be true. From this conclusion, the rest of the claims follow easily. Since the interpretations are based upon the theory, the theoretical hypotheses are confirmed. The confirmatory evidence has been obtained by following the psychoanalytic method of investigation. Hence, the validity of the method is also established by the same criterion. Unlike the evidential rigor that is so essential in all other scientific discipline, the Tally Argument can prove all the major theoretical claims of psychoanalysis, including the validity of its method of investigation, simply by appeal to its unique therapeutic success. "Magnificent, if true!" exclaims Grünbaum (*Foundations*, p. 141).

Grünbaum claims that the Tally Argument is the most plausible formulation of Freud's defence against the suggestibility charge. The crucial question regarding Grünbaum's reconstruction, of course, is whether Freud himself believed in the truth of NCT. Grünbaum gives the following reason to show that Freud was driven to postulate NCT and, therefore, he must have believed it to be true: Freud needed to postulate NCT in order to explain the difference in the therapeutic outcome of Breuer's cathartic method, and his own modification of the method, which employed free association.

After experiencing therapeutic failure with Breuer's cathartic method, Freud postulated conditions of adequacy for a traumatic event to be a suitable determinant of the symptom in question. These conditions of adequacy are: (i) the traumatic event must be relevantly suitable to be a determinant of the symptom in question; and (ii) it must possess the necessary traumatic force to produce the symptom. Freud then showed that the events with which the symptoms started failed to meet one or both the conditions of adequacy in the majority of cases. Hence, these events were reduced to the status of "precipitating causes" or "occasioning causes" while Freud contended that there were earlier traumas that were definitely pathogenic. This was the beginning of the formulation of NCT. Insight into the causal mechanism of symptoms will involve the unearthing of those earlier traumas that the individual experienced in his or her childhood. The NCT would explain the therapeutic failures and successes in the following way: cases ending in unfavourable therapeutic gain merely removed the precipitating or occasioning trauma. In therapeutically successful cases, the analysis went beyond the occasioning trauma, resulting in the patient's insight into the causal mechanism of the symptom. The traumas in such cases were genuinely pathologically operative—that is, they satisfied the two conditions of adequacy.

Grünbaum claims that the correctness of this interpretation can be corroborated by the fact that Freud considered as counterexamples those few cases where the occasioning trauma did meet the conditions of adequacy laid down by him. He cautions that therapeutic gain to be had merely by analysing the precipitating cause will not be durable. Clearly, he is invoking his NCT here. NCT was needed again to explain the capricious results Freud obtained by the use of the hypnotic method. His contention that hypnotic therapy merely leads to symptom substitution rather than cure is intelligible only in the perspective of his belief in NCT. It is insight alone that could bring about a real cure. Treatment by hypnosis does not lead to insight and hence to a durable cure.

One might argue against this formulation of Grünbaum's by pointing out that Freud could not have believed in NCT after he was forced to retract his seduction aetiology of hysteria, because he was convinced later that some of these incidents never took place. Thus, in such cases, to claim that a cure had occurred by insight would be a genuine counterexample to NCT. This would imply that a permanent cure had occurred by gaining pseudo-insight into an event that had never occurred at all. Grünbaum's reply to this objection is that if patients were cured by gaining pseudo-insight through their analysis into the episodes of sexual abuse that never occurred that would have really disconfirmed NCT.

But such cures never occurred. In a letter written to Fliess in 1897, the very first reason that Freud gives for abandoning seduction aetiology of hysteria was that no noticeable therapeutic success in conquering the underlying neuroses of the patients could be achieved. Whatever little success was achieved could have been "wrought by Suggestion" (see *Foundations*, p. 159). Grünbaum quotes from Freud's letter to Fliess in which Freud expresses his disappointment at the failure of the cathartic method and the running away of his "most favourably inclined patients" (*Foundations*, p. 159) and lack of complete success. Thus, Grünbaum argues that even the debacle of the seduction aetiology did not gainsay the NCT.

The second argument of Freud

According to Grünbaum, the Tally Argument is the best defence of psychoanalysis against the suggestibility charge in the entire psychoanalytic literature. In the same lecture ("Analytic therapy") Freud proposed another argument to rebut the suggestibility charge. Grünbaum argues that this second argument is circular. I relate my own formulation of the argument below:

(1) Treatment gains obtained through suggestion last only as long as the state of suggestibility of P towards his or her therapist is maintained.
(2) Thus, a continued state of dependence of P towards the therapist is a necessary condition for the maintenance of treatment gains through suggestion.
(3) In a successful analytic treatment the state of suggestibility of P (transference) is resolved at the end of the therapy.
(4) If cure persists beyond this state of suggestibility of P towards the therapist, then cure is not due to suggestion.
(5) In a large number of cases, the cure persists even after P has overcome his or her state of suggestibility towards the therapist.

Conclusion: the success of analytic therapy is not due to suggestion.

If a favourable therapeutic outcome results due to transference, it will disappear when the transference is resolved. In other words, the therapeutic outcome due to suggestion will last only while the state of suggestibility lasts. With its disappearance, the "cure" also disappears.

It is clear that Freud here is appealing to the durability of the cure beyond the state of transference as a proof that the cure is not due to suggestion. In my own formulation of Freud's argument in the next chapter, I shall utilise an amended version of this argument. Grünbaum objects that the above argument is viciously circular because resolution of the transference is achieved by convincing the patient of the real origin of his or her transference attitude; namely, of his or her earliest object-attachments during the repressed period of childhood. Resolution of transference is based upon two theoretical hypotheses: (i) Transference is the product of the earliest object attachments during the repressed period of childhood. (ii) This transference is resolved by the patient's gaining insight into the causal mechanism of transference.

The justification of the two theoretical hypotheses above is obtained by clinical data. But clinical data are supposed to be contaminated from the very beginning. Therefore, the second argument offered by Freud tries to answer the charge of spurious confirmation of psychoanalytical hypotheses by appealing to hypotheses whose confirmatory status is similarly doubtful. Thus, the argument is viciously circular. Therefore, it is chiefly the NCT on which Freud could rely for the validation of his main aetiological claims. Since NCT is also the best defence of psychoanalysis against the suggestibility charge in Grünbaum's opinion, the confirmatory status of the theoretical hypotheses of psychoanalysis largely depends on the soundness of this argument.

Now we come to the crucial question. Is the Tally Argument sound? Can it successfully play the dual role it has been formulated to perform; namely, to prove that the results of psychoanalytic therapy are not due to suggestion and that the data confirming the psychoanalytic hypotheses are free from the contamination of suggestion? Grünbaum says that it is on the basis of NCT that Freud could claim the authenticity of his clinical data. Hence, to the extent that Freud disavowed NCT in later years, he also relinquished his reliance on the sole argument with the help of which he could authenticate his clinical data and his psychoanalytic method of inquiry. Also, currently available empirical information regarding the non-effectiveness of psychoanalytical therapy in effecting "real cures" makes the status of NCT dubious. Freudian theory, thus, is devoid of any logical vindication both of its theory and its therapy (see *Foundations*, pp. 159–160). Grünbaum proceeds to cite evidence from both fronts. I shall present his evidence below.

Grünbaum claims that there are at least two prominent disclaimers by Freud about the therapeutic efficacy of a psychoanalytic method of treatment: one in his 1937 paper "Analysis terminable and interminable" and another in 1926 (see *Foundations*, p. 160). In 1937, Freud repudiated the therapeutic efficacy of psychoanalytic treatment and confined it essentially to palliative effects. He pointed out that psychoanalytic therapeutic success is not even prophylactic and does not guarantee against the re-emergence of the symptom. This admission proves NCT false. Even if NCT were true, it would have needed empirical evidence for its own validation, but the disclaimer from Freud was devastating for his theory. With the support of NCT gone, Freud is left virtually without any defence for the empirical credibility of his theory.

A consequence of NCT is that Freud could not believe in spontaneous remissions of neuroses. In 1926 Freud admits that there can be spontaneous remission of neuroses and that psychoanalytical therapy does nothing more than effect the cure of those neuroses, which would have been cured by themselves (without therapeutic intervention) anyway. Thus, by his own evidence, Freud had no vindication for his theory.

NCT is discredited if it can be shown that insight is not a necessary condition for cure. There are rival therapies that have successfully achieved "all round improvement" in the personality of patients or cures without giving the patient insight into the causal mechanism of his or her symptoms (see *Foundations*, p. 161). Even some prominent analysts have admitted that all round improvement in the personality of a patient has been brought about with rival therapies of psychoanalysis. Grünbaum defines a therapy as a rival therapy if the rationale, dynamics or methods of treatment of the therapy are different from those of psychoanalysis.

Comparative studies, according to Grünbaum, fail to substantiate any superior therapeutic gain for psychoanalysis. But if the therapeutic gain of a psychoanalytical treatment is not superior to those of other modalities of treatment, then it is reasonable, though not compelling, to interpret its therapeutic gains as placebo effects. It is possible that all the therapeutic gains by all forms of psychotherapy are placebo effects. Psychologist Jerome Frank suggests that all forms of psychotherapy treat their patients by giving them support. Prioleau, Murdock and Brody (1983) point out that there is no significant difference between the effects of any form of psychotherapy and treatment by placebo. Under the weight of this evidence, Freud's NCT breaks down completely.

Freud made a distinction between mere symptom cure and a radical cure of neuroses. He and his followers even today claim that their therapy, as contrasted with other forms of therapy, is a causal therapy. In his 1917 "Analytic therapy" lecture, Freud qualified the sense in which psychoanalytic therapy is a causal therapy. While admitting that psychoanalytic treatment undertakes a more thoroughgoing attack on neuroses, he pointed out that it does not go to the root of the symptoms; namely, the constitutional factors of P that made him or her vulnerable to neurosis in the first place. Some kind of chemical therapy altering a patient's constitutional factors would be the true causal therapy. Grünbaum contends that so long as Freud's aetiologies are not validated, psychoanalytic therapy is not a causal therapy in any sense of the term.

One important point needs to be mentioned in this connection. It has been especially difficult for the Freudians to cope with the results of behaviour therapy. A successful behaviour therapy is a counterexample to Freudian aetiologic hypotheses. According to Freudian hypothesis, a neurotic symptom is a product of an underlying conflict. To remove the symptom, the conflict must be removed. But in case of a successful behaviour therapy, the symptom is removed without any acknowledgement of the conflict. In all such cases, Freud would say that the symptom removal would not be lasting. Fisher and Greenberg have summarised the results of a study that shows that lasting results have been obtained from behaviour therapy (see Fisher & Greenberg, 1978, pp. 427–435).

Some Freudians, in order to explain this phenomenon, made a distinction between "ghost" and "non-ghost" symptoms. They explained that the underlying conflict of some symptoms can be resolved by spontaneous ego maturation, but due to sheer inertia of habit, symptoms can be maintained. But this distinction of symptoms suffers from the following serious difficulties:

- It invokes spontaneous remission and this goes against NCT—the main pillar of defence of psychoanalysis against the charge of suggestibility. Not only that, NCT is needed to explain the concept of symptom substitution so frequently resorted to by Freud and Freudians.
- It cuts a vital link that was necessary for Breuer and Freud in order to arrive at their clinical aetiologies. An ongoing repression, according to

them, was a necessary condition for the persistence of the symptom. But if a cure can occur without the lifting of repression, then an ongoing repression is no longer required for the maintenance of the symptoms. Freudians would have difficulty explaining why, in some cases, symptoms persist when they do. Thus, this distinction tries to save the theory by cutting a vital link essential for any formulation of the psychoanalytic aetiological hypothesis.

- This explanation makes psychoanalytic therapy largely superfluous. It is applicable only to those cases where the symptoms are non-ghost symptoms. Large numbers of people who have better ego strength will take recourse to short-term therapies, avoiding the enormously time-consuming and expensive psychoanalytical therapy.

The above evidence severely undercut the legitimacy of the Tally Argument and thus the efficacy of the dual role it was supposed to play. With the support of the Tally Argument gone and with no alternative argument in sight to restore the epistemic reliability of the clinical data, the therapeutic success of psychoanalytical treatment must be considered placebo effect.

Grünbaum does not rest content merely to argue that it is in principle possible for the clinical data to be contaminated by the suggestive influence of the analyst. He painstakingly points out some alleged instances from the writings of Freud to prove that the clinical data were actually contaminated; that Freud required a kind of memory and felt entitled on theoretical grounds to hector the patient relentlessly for not having retrieved the desired sort of memory (See *Foundations*, p. 151). Assuming that the argument is supposed to apply to the present status of psychoanalysis also, one may reasonably conclude that Grünbaum is directing similar objections against analytical sessions in general. Thus, his objections claim to be both methodological and empirical.

Grünbaum cautions us not to ignore the intimate role that therapeutic success has played in the validation of psychoanalysis. He points out that even those psychoanalytic hypotheses that are not directly related to the therapy, or to the dynamics of the therapy, are still "epistemically parasitic" on positive therapeutic results. He claims that Freud has essentially relied on NCT to "vindicate the probity of clinical data" and this fact is largely overlooked (See *Foundations*, p. 167).

Grünbaum contends that Freud's formulation of NCT brings to relief his image as a sophisticated methodologist. But once he stopped relying on his NCT, he inconsistently still believed in the authenticity of the clinical data, forgetting that without the support of NCT the suggestibility problem haunts the epistemic credibility of the clinical data. With the demise of the Tally Argument, psychoanalysis faces an epistemic liability of enormous proportion.

The significance of Grünbaum's suggestibility charge is deeper than it appears. We are posed with the serious problem as to whether any aetiological hypothesis can be confirmed without rigorously controlled experiments and whether and to what extent introspection of a subject can confirm a causal hypothesis about his or her own mental states. The Tally Argument, as reconstructed by Grünbaum, is certainly unsound. But we are faced with the following question: Did Freud really assert the claim made in the Tally Argument? We shall deal with the question in the next chapter.

CHAPTER THREE

The ghost of suggestibility

Section I

Did Freud really subscribe to NCT?

The Tally Argument of Grünbaum may be characterised as an historical argument. It is a reconstruction of an argument allegedly given by Freud and is based upon "historical evidence"; namely, textual evidence. However, the functional importance of the Tally Argument is not confined merely to the clarification of Freud's ideas. Grünbaum has used the Tally Argument as representative of the best defence of psychoanalysis against the suggestibility charge. From this point of view, the Tally Argument is related to the present theoretical status of psychoanalysis as well. Our evaluation of this argument, therefore, will involve both these aspects—that is, whether the argument correctly represents the view of Freud, and whether it is compatible with the theoretical implications of psychoanalysis. However, very often consideration of the first question will involve the consideration of the second question. I shall, therefore, merge the two questions together and evaluate both aspects of the Tally Argument in one context.

Our evaluation of an argument is generally related to the consideration of its logical validity and soundness. In the case of a reconstructed argument, one more consideration is added to the above two; namely, the historical accuracy of the reconstructed argument. This last consideration is independent of the logical validity or soundness of the argument. A reconstructed argument may be logically valid and sound but it may not represent the view of the philosopher whose argument it claims to be. It is customary, therefore, to provide justification for the reconstructed argument. This justification is often derived from various sources. Chief among these sources is textual evidence; compatibility with the general structure of the theory believed by the philosopher in question; and relevance of the argument for the system of the philosopher in question.

It is possible to provide sufficient justification for any argument if textual evidence provides support to the reconstruction. However, textual evidence alone is often considered insufficient for the purposes of justification of a reconstructed argument, because it is possible to give a different interpretation to textual evidence. If textual evidence is supported by the logical implications of the theory and/or its relevance for the system of the philosopher in question, the reconstruction acquires greater strength.

Grünbaum has largely relied on textual evidence and the relevance of the argument for Freudian theory. In this and the following sections, I shall examine Grünbaum's evidence for the justification of the Tally Argument and show that attribution of this argument to Freud is unjustified. In order to perform this task, I shall follow the following procedure:

- I shall produce extensive textual evidence that will contradict the logical consequences or the premise/s of the Tally Argument, thus showing that Freud did not subscribe to the NCT. I shall also examine Grünbaum's textual evidence and point out its inadequacy to support his argument.
- I shall show that the logical consequences of the NCT are incompatible with some of the logical consequences of the psychoanalytic theory. This will serve to show that even if Freud subscribed to NCT, the argument cannot be applied to evaluate the status of psychoanalysis in general.
- I shall show that NCT is not logically indispensable for the theoretical structure of psychoanalysis, as claimed by Grünbaum. The reasons he has given for Freud's belief in NCT do not necessitate such a belief.

The present section is mostly concerned with the question of textual evidence providing justification for the Tally Argument.

The NCT is a conjunction of two premises. The first premise states that the psychoanalytic method of interpretation, etc. is a necessary condition for gaining insight into the causal mechanism of one's neurotic symptom. The second conjunct states that this insight is a necessary condition for the cure of one's neurosis. By "cure" it is meant a durable cure and not merely a cure in the sense of symptom substitution. The NCT can be given at least two plausible interpretations. I shall state both these interpretations and show that neither of them was subscribed to by Freud.

The first interpretation of NCT, in its strictly logical sense, provides us with the following consequences:

(1) No physico-chemical or even constitutional change, if it is possible to bring it about, would be able to bring about the desired therapeutic state in P. If insight is a necessary condition for the cure of the symptoms, then even physico-chemical changes cannot effect a cure.
(2) Methods of treatment other then psychoanalysis would bring about only symptomatic relief of P.
(3) Spontaneous remission of P's neurosis is not possible.

It may be pointed out that NCT does not rule out physico-chemical changes brought about by insight. It is possible that the causal sequence in the cure of a neurosis is the following: if insight, then physico-chemical changes, then cure. However, this sequence does not invalidate point (1) above, which directly follows from the first premise of NCT; namely, the psychoanalytic method of interpretations, etc. is a necessary condition for gaining insight into the causal mechanism of one's symptom formation. In other words, to say that insight is a necessary condition for the cure of a neurosis is to claim that no durable cure of a symptom is possible without insight. Grünbaum has given this strong interpretation to "necessary condition". Grünbaum derives (2) and (3) from the Tally Argument as shown in the following passage:

> Clearly, NCT entails not only that there is no spontaneous remission of psychoneuroses but also that, if there are any cures at all, psychoanalysis is *uniquely* therapeutic for such disorders as compared to any *rival* therapies. (*Foundations*, p. 140)

If Freud did believe in NCT, as Grünbaum claims, then in order to be consistent he should believe in all three logical consequences of NCT;

namely, the inefficacy of physico-chemical changes, rival therapies and spontaneous remission to bring about a cure.

I shall show that there is ample historical (textual) evidence that Freud neither believed in Grünbaum's NCT or its logical consequences. As Grünbaum himself agrees, for Freud, repression merely constitutes a necessary and not a sufficient condition for the formation of symptom S. In fact, even today we do not know what these sufficient conditions are. According to Freud, all manifestations of neurotic symptoms are overdetermined. Multiple causal factors must operate to bring about the formation of a neurotic illness. Removal of any of the necessary conditions could result in a positive therapeutic gain. How important the therapeutic gain is depends upon the importance of the role the causal factor has played in the genesis of the symptom.

However, in addition to the psychological mechanisms, Freud repeatedly mentioned the constitutional factors of P as some of the most important necessary conditions in the illness of P. As early as 1896, he says:

> ... for the physician cannot set himself the task of altering a constitution such as the hysterical one. He must content himself with getting rid of the troubles to which such a constitution is inclined and which may arise from it with the conjunction of external circumstances. (Freud, 1895d, p. 262)

Regarding psychoneuroses in general, he says:

> The expectation that every neurotic phenomenon can be cured may, I suspect, be derived from the layman's belief that the neuroses are something quite unnecessary which have no right whatever to exist. Whereas in fact they are severe, constitutionally fixed illnesses, which rarely restrict themselves to only a few attacks but persist as a rule over long periods or throughout life. Our analytic experience ... has led us to neglect the constitutional factor in our therapeutic practice, and in any case we can do nothing about it; but in theory we ought always to bear it in mind. (Freud, 1933a, pp. 153–154)

There are other repeated references to the role the constitutional factors play in the manifestation of neurotic illness (see Freud 1896a). Indeed, it is not possible to list all the references to heredity factors as one of the necessary conditions of neuroses as explicated by Freud. If this is the case, removal of the constitutional factors would result in therapeutic gain. In fact, as the above passage shows, Freud considered constitutional factors to be one of the most important causal factors in neuroses. Freud even asserts that bringing about such changes may be considered the true causal therapy of neuroses. As he says:

> Supposing, now, that it was possible, by some chemical means, perhaps, to interfere in this chemical mechanism, to increase or decrease the quantity of libido present at a given time or to strengthen one instinct at the cost of another—this then would be a causal therapy in the true sense of the word, for which our analysis would have carried out the indispensable preliminary work of reconnaissance. (Freud, 1916–1917, p. 436)

In 1916–1917, when Freud wrote this passage, bringing about such constitutional changes was a matter of theoretical possibility only. But today with the increasing knowledge of human physiology and genetic engineering, it is more than a mere theoretical possibility. Thus, Freud does not deny that such physiological changes, if they can be implemented, would lead to a permanent cure of the neuroses of P. In another place, he says:

> Today organic physical methods of treating neurotic states need scarcely be mentioned. Analysis as a psycho-therapeutic procedure does not stand in opposition to other methods used in this specialized branch of medicine; it does not diminish their value nor exclude them. There is no theoretical inconsistency in a doctor who likes to call himself a psychotherapist using analysis on his patients alongside of any other method of treatment according to the peculiarities of the case and the favourable or unfavourable external circumstances. (Freud, 1933a, p. 152)

All these passages unambiguously establish that Freud believed that cure of neurotic symptoms could be brought about by suitable constitutional or physico-chemical changes if it was possible. The last quoted passage was written in 1933. By that time some advance had been made in controlling some psychological symptoms with the help of physico-chemical therapy. However, so long as this alternative is not available, psychotherapy remains the only means of effecting a cure of neuroses. These assertions are clear counterexamples to Grünbaum's claim that Freud believed in his NCT.

How can Grünbaum reconcile these passages with the claims of NCT? There are two possible replies that Grünbaum can make in response to the above. The first is Freud's belief that the therapeutic efficacy of physiological or chemical changes is the result of his progressive dissatisfaction with psychoanalytic therapy. This objection can easily be answered. It is to be noted that Grünbaum does not specify at what point Freud became dissatisfied with the therapeutic efficacy of psychoanalysis, if at all he did. He, however, says that Freud believed in NCT at least until 1917. If this is the case, then at least until 1917 Freud should not have advocated the therapeutic efficacy of any method—physical or psychological—other than psychoanalytic. But this is not the case. Passages relating to the importance of constitutional factors can be found from beginning to end of Freud's theoretical development. The passage in which he characterises physico-chemical therapy as the true "causal" therapy was written in the same year (1917) and is part of Lecture XXVII of the same lecture series on which Grünbaum has based his NCT.

In fact, in Lecture XXIII of the same lecture series Freud states clearly:

> Thus fixation of the libido in the adult, which we introduced into the aetiological equation of neurosis as representing the constitutional factor [p. 346], now falls, for our purposes, into two further parts: the inherited constitution and the disposition acquired in early childhood. (Freud, 1917, p. 362)

Freud says in as clear terms as possible that a neurosis is produced by a combination of constitutional factors and later experiences, and a physician cannot alter the constitutional factors (1895d, p. 262). In other words, he considers both these factors necessary for the formation of a neurotic symptom. In Lecture XXVII (1916–1917) he also asserts the importance of physico-chemical changes as being the true causal therapy. How can he then propound NCT in Lecture XXVIII ("Analytic therapy"), asserting that insight alone can remove the neurotic symptom? This explanation, therefore, fails to save Grünbaum's position.

Another way in which Grünbaum may try to explain these passages is simply by claiming that Freud was inconsistent. He inconsistently maintained the claim made in these passages while believing in NCT. This is a serious charge and Grünbaum has given no evidence that such is the case. In fact, Grünbaum has neglected even to mention these passages. Later in this section, I shall show how these passages are in harmony with the general structure of Freud's theory while NCT is not. Grünbaum, however, may object to my interpretation of NCT. He might say that his NCT is not to be given such strict logical interpretation.

The Necessary Condition Thesis should be read with the following consideration in mind: that since the means were not available to influence constitutional or physico-chemical factors in the treatment of neuroses, they are left out of consideration in the formation of the Tally Argument. In other words, the domain of the applicability of the Tally Argument is restricted to psychotherapies of all forms only and the NCT should be interpreted accordingly. Thus, we should read the NCT with the following qualifications in mind:

> Given that psychotherapies are the only means to effect cures of psychoneuroses: (1) the psychoanalytical method of interpretations, etc. is necessary to gain insight into the unconscious causal mechanism of one's neurotic symptoms; (2) this insight is a necessary condition for the cure of P's neurotic symptoms.

According to this second interpretation, which we shall refer to as NCT′, the only logical consequences are the impossibility of cure by methods of treatment other than psychoanalysis and the impossibility of spontaneous remission, which are mentioned at the beginning of this section. It is possible that Grünbaum has NCT′ in mind because he does not even mention that physico-chemical changes cannot effect a cure as the logical consequence of NCT. I shall now show that there is ample textual evidence that Freud did not believe that methods of treatment other than psychoanalysis always bring about only symptomatic relief to P and thought that spontaneous remissions were not possible and hence did not believe in NCT′. This discussion will show that Freud was not inconsistent.

Grünbaum states that as per NCT′ the psychoanalytic method of treatment is the only method that can bring about a cure of P's neurosis. Grünbaum does derive this conclusion explicitly as stated in the second conclusion of his Tally Argument and attributes it to Freud. I shall show that Freud could not have subscribed to this view. As early as 1905 Freud states:

> There are many ways and means of practising psychotherapy. All that lead to recovery are good ... We have developed the technique of hypnotic suggestion, and psychotherapy by distraction, by exercise, and by eliciting suitable affects. *I despise none of these methods and would use them all in appropriate circumstances.* If I have actually come to confine myself to one form of treatment, to the method which Breuer called *cathartic*, but which I myself prefer to call "analytic", it is because I have allowed myself to be influenced by purely subjective motives. (my emphasis) (Freud, 1905a, p. 259)

This statement is certainly not consistent with the view Grünbaum has attributed to Freud in his second conjunct of NCT′. In this passage Freud speaks of a number of psychotherapeutic methods and contends that different methods may be suitable for different patients according to the peculiarities of their symptoms and personalities. In fact, he does not even deny that a complete cure of a psychogenic disorder is possible due to simple religious faith. In an article written in the same year, he states:

> It would be convenient but quite wrong, simply to refuse all credence to these miraculous cures and to seek to explain the accounts of them as a combination of pious fraud and inaccurate observation. Though an explanation of this kind may often be justified, it is not enough to enable us to dismiss entirely the fact of miraculous cure. They do really occur and have occurred at every period of history. And they concern not merely illnesses of mental origins—those, that is, which are based on "imagination" and are therefore likely to be especially affected by the circumstances of a pilgrimage—but also illnesses with an "organic" basis which had previously resisted all the efforts of physicians. (Freud, 1905a, p. 290)

What he refused to believe was that such cures are "miraculous" in nature. In the continuing passages he gives his account of how the cure must have taken place. The theoretical account may or may not be acceptable, but that is not relevant to the point I am making. The point to be emphasised here is that these passages distinctly and clearly show the fallacy Grünbaum has committed in attributing NCT′ to Freud.

Unless there is evidence that at some point between 1896 and 1917 Freud changed his mind regarding the question under consideration, the second conjunct of NCT′ simply cannot be accepted as a Freudian proposition. Grünbaum has not provided any such evidence. I shall provide below evidence to the contrary. In a passage written in 1932 Freud essentially reiterates what he had said in 1905:

> I have told you psychoanalysis began as a method of treatment; but I did not want to commend it to your interest as a method of treatment but on account of the truths it contains … *As a method of treatment it is one among many, though to be sure,* [my emphasis] *primus inter pares*. (Freud, 1933a, p. 157)

If these passages are any indication, there seems to be a continuity of belief regarding the therapeutic role of psychoanalytic method from the beginning of Freud's career to the end. This passage was written in 1932 and, as we know, Freud died in 1939. It was considered one among many methods of treatment available, though Freud did consider it the most effective of all. The last claim may or may not be true but it is far from claiming that psychoanalysis is uniquely therapeutic for the cure of neurotic symptoms.

Grünbaum may have two possible replies to the above:

(1) The above passages are not inconsistent with (NCT′) if the phrase "most effective form of treatment" is given the following interpretation:
A psychoanalytic method of treatment is the most effective among all psychological methods of treatment because it alone is capable of bringing about a permanent or durable cure that is not a symptom substitution. All other methods lead merely to a recovery, which is a form of symptom substitution.

This interpretation does not deny that there are other methods of psychological treatment for neurotic symptoms and that they lead to recovery, but it denies that any one of them is sufficiently effective to bring about a permanent cure. Since NCT′ refers only to a permanent cure, these passages are not inconsistent with the claim of NCT′.

If this interpretation is correct, Freud would not have asserted the truth of the so-called "miraculous cure". Here he does use the word "cure" in the sense of permanent cure. As Grünbaum himself points out, Freud has repeatedly asserted that the results of suggestive treatment were capricious. It is not that no case was successfully treated with hypnotism but that no one understood why in some cases the treatment was followed by success while in others it was not (See *Foundations*, p. 140). NCT′ requires that not even a single case could be or had been cured by the method of hypnotic suggestion or by any other method of treatment. That is why Grünbaum has taken pains to deny that Freud's so-called case of successful treatment by hypnotism constitutes a counterexample to his assertion that Freud did believe in NCT′. I will later show why to be theoretically consistent Freud could not deny that permanent cures could be effected by methods other than psychoanalytic treatment. And this assertion is not inconsistent with the claim that psychoanalytic treatment is the most effective form of treatment for neurotic symptoms. Thus, we conclude that the phrase "most effective form of treatment" does not save Grünbaum's position.

(2) The second reply that Grünbaum could offer is to refer to a change of belief on the part of Freud about the therapeutic efficacy of psychoanalytic treatment. However, Grünbaum does not give any date reference regarding this change of belief. He merely asserts that at least till 1917 Freud believed in the NCT′. The lecture "Explanation, Application and Orientation" was written in 1932. Freud's assertion regarding psychoanalytic therapy in that lecture may just be an indication of his loss of faith in the efficacy of psychoanalytic therapy.

It is difficult to counter this objection. The nature of the objection has drastically limited the scope of falsifying it with the help of textual evidence. Grünbaum formulates the Tally Argument on the basis of a lecture given in 1917 and ascribes a change of belief to Freud later than 1917. Without any definite date reference involved in this ascription, any textual evidence later than 1917 that is contrary to Grünbaum's assertion is liable to be interpreted as a reflection of Freud's changed attitude regarding the therapeutic efficacy of psychoanalytic treatment. Thus, twenty-two years of Freud's mature life and work become unusable to contradict the claim Grünbaum has attributed to him. However, to counteract this limitation imposed by the imprecision of the argument, I shall adopt the following strategy that if any given article, in general, does not show a lack of confidence in the psychoanalytic theory or method of treatment, I shall accept it as evidence of Freud's continued faith in his theory and therapy.

Given the above strategy, the lecture "Explanation, Application and Orientation" itself is one of the best examples of Freud's belief in the truth of his theory and therapy. The lecture is devoted to the development of measures to apply psychoanalysis in the wider area of anthropology, education, and child development. Freud would not have advocated such application if he had lost faith in the truth of his theory and the efficacy of his therapy. Thus, the passage in question cannot be explained by Grünbaum's objection. Freud clearly states in the same lecture:

> Compared with the other psychotherapeutic procedures psychoanalysis is beyond any doubt the most powerful. It is just and fair, too, that this should be so for it is also the most laborious and time-consuming; it would not be used on slight cases. In suitable cases it is possible by its means to get rid of disturbances and bring about changes for which in pre-analytic times one would not have ventured to hope. (Freud, 1933a, p. 153)

He admits the limitations of psychoanalytic therapy due to the practice of psychotherapy in diluted form by many psychoanalysts, but defends the therapy against the charge of being extremely time-consuming:

> But I shall be still more sorry if you were to think it is my intention to lower your opinion of psycho-analysis as a therapy. Perhaps I really made a clumsy start. For I wanted to do the opposite: to excuse the therapeutic limitations of analysis by pointing out their inevitability. With the same aim in view I turn to another point: the reproach against analytical treatment that it takes a disproportionately long time. On this it must be said that psychical changes do in fact only take place slowly; if they occur rapidly, suddenly, that is a bad sign. (Freud, 1933a, p. 156)

I conclude, therefore, that in the historical development of Freud's theoretical beliefs, there is strong evidence that contradicts Grünbaum's ascription of NCT′ to Freud. It is to be noted that if Freud did not believe in the second conjunct of NCT′ and did not derive the second conclusion of the Tally Argument (that only analytic treatment could have wrought the conquest of P's psychoneurosis) Grünbaum's subsequent attempt to falsify NCT′ by citing examples of cures achieved by other methods of therapy becomes irrelevant. It remains incumbent on me, however, to explain these cures in accordance with psychoanalytic theory—a task I shall take up later in this chapter.

Before we take up the point that, according to Freud, spontaneous remissions of neuroses are impossible, it will be in order to examine Grünbaum's evidence for ascribing conclusion two of the Tally Argument to Freud. Here's what Grünbaum says:

> I have called attention to two conclusions that follow from the premises of Freud's Tally Argument. … *But Freud himself explicitly deduced only the first of these two conclusions*, and stated the second separately in the same 1917 paper …
>
> … he tells us (S. E., 1917, 16: 458) that therapeutic successes of analysis are not only "second to none of the finest in the field of internal medicine" but also that psychoanalytic treatment gains "could not have been achieved by any other procedure", let alone spontaneously. (my emphasis) (*Foundations*, p. 142)

This constitutes all of Grünbaum's evidence for ascribing conclusion two of the Tally Argument to Freud.

Let us examine the evidence in its proper context. The statement "… we achieve, under favourable conditions, successes which are second to none in the field of internal medicine" was made in Lecture XVI of the same series of lectures on which Grünbaum has based his Tally Argument. The proper context of making this statement is the following: Freud states that psychoanalytic therapy has failed to effect a cure in cases of paranoid delusion. His statement is clear and without any tinge of hesitation. He says:

> As you know, our psychiatric therapy is not hitherto able to influence delusions. Is it possible that psychoanalysis can do so, thanks to its insight into the mechanism of these symptoms? No, Gentlemen, it cannot. It is as powerless (for the time being at least) against these ailments as any other forms of therapy. (Freud, 1916–1917, p. 255)

This may be a limitation of its therapeutic efficacy, but this limitation should not throw a negative light on what the therapy has achieved. As he says:

> Let me therefore end my remarks to-day by informing you that there are extensive groups of nervous disorders in which the

> transformation of our better understanding into therapeutic power has actually taken place, and that in these illnesses, which are difficult of access by other means, we achieve, under favourable conditions, successes which are second to no others in the field of internal medicine. (Freud, 1916–1917, pp. 255–256)

Read in this context, the statement simply claims that there are many nervous disorders that have been found to be difficult to cure by the "existing" methods of treatment and in these areas psychoanalysis has done at least as well as other successful methods of treatment.

If we now add to this claim the later assertion that these successes "could not have been achieved by any other procedure", the new claim should be read in the following way: in those extensive groups of nervous disorders that have been found to be difficult to access by other existing methods of treatment, psychoanalysis has done at least as well as any other successful method and these successes could not be achieved by any other procedures. This addition, in fact, does not add much to the old claim, which has already stated that these groups of nervous disorders were difficult to cure by existing methods of treatment. During Freud's time, these methods of treatment were by hypnosis, hydrotherapy, rest cure, etc. Compared to these forms of therapy, psychoanalysis had genuinely come up with a form of therapy that for the first time dealt with the emotions and conflicts of the patients and helped them in the process. Since other methods mentioned above did not apply these treatment processes, patients were not accessible to them and hence cure in such cases where psychoanalysis has been successful could not have been achieved. This is a far cry from claiming that if P is cured of his neurosis, he must have been treated by psychoanalysis. The textual evidence Grünbaum cites is taken out of context and given a distorted interpretation.

Let us now come to the point made by Grünbaum that Freud did not believe that spontaneous remissions of neuroses are possible. NCT′ implies that spontaneous cures of neuroses are not possible. Ascribing this belief to Freud, Grünbaum goes on to falsify it by citing textual evidence that Freud, later on, admitted that spontaneous cures do occur—an assertion that goes on to contradict and undermine NCT′. Also, there is empirical evidence that spontaneous cures do occur in psychoneuroses. This empirical evidence also goes against Freud, if he believed in NCT′, as claimed by Grünbaum. Some clarification is essential in order to understand Freud's view about spontaneous remission of neuroses and the claim made by Grünbaum.

The first important point to keep in mind is that to claim that a neurosis has been cured spontaneously is not to claim that the cure was uncaused. It merely implies that the cure has occurred due to causes unrelated to therapeutic intervention. The claim that spontaneous remission of neuroses is not possible is vague and can be given a number of possible interpretations. The claim may be expressed more precisely in the following way: according to Freud, there is no case of psychoneurosis that is cured spontaneously. If this is also Grünbaum's case and this is also implied by NCT', then it is obviously false. If we interpret the term "psychoneuroses" in an unqualified sense, textual evidence unambiguously supports the view that Freud believed that spontaneous remission of psychoneuroses can and does occur. The first reference to spontaneous cure of neuroses is found in 1896:

> It may be objected that, in cases of hysteria like this, in which illness has run its course, the residual symptoms in any case pass away spontaneously. It may be said in reply, however, that a spontaneous cure of this kind is very often neither rapid nor complete enough and that it can be assisted to an extraordinary degree by our therapeutic intervention. We may readily leave it for the moment as an unresolved question whether by means of the cathartic therapy we cure only what is capable of spontaneous cure or sometimes also what would not have cleared up spontaneously. (Freud, 1895d, p. 263)

This passage clearly indicates that Freud was aware that some psychoneuroses are amenable to spontaneous remission. He is claiming that such a cure could be hastened and made more complete with therapeutic intervention. There is no inconsistency in this claim. The common uncomplicated cold is often cured spontaneously but it is possible to hasten the process by taking, say, vitamin C tables.

Psychologically speaking, in the process of growing up, childhood and adolescence are considered two critical periods—childhood because of the immaturity of the ego and adolescence because of the intense physiological changes and consequent emotional upheaval the ego has to cope with. During these periods, it is not uncommon for young people to pass through a phase of neuroses that are often cured spontaneously. I quote:

> Since we have learnt how to look more sharply, we are tempted to say that neurosis in children is not the exception but the rule, as though it could scarcely be avoided on the path from the innate disposition of infancy to civilized society. In most cases this neurotic phase in childhood is overcome spontaneously. (Freud, 1926e, p. 215)

Freud has made similar remarks about adolescence also. In the case of Wolf Man, he explicitly states that the patient's religious obsession of years' standing was cured spontaneously. Freud says:

> I have formed the opinion that this case, like many others which clinical psychiatry has labelled with the most multifarious and shifting diagnoses, is to be regarded as a condition following on an obsessional neurosis which has come to an end *spontaneously* [my italics], but has left a defect behind it after recovery. (Freud, 1918b, p. 8)

These passages clearly indicate that Freud never denied the possibility of spontaneous cure of neuroses, in some cases at least. How then can Grünbaum claim otherwise?

It is possible that Grünbaum is making a different claim. To understand his claim clearly, let us examine the evidence on which Grünbaum's claim is based. As evidence for his claim Grünbaum cites some textual references. I quote from *Foundations*:

> He (Freud) reiterated his distinction between a psychoanalytic "radical cure" of a full-fledged neurosis and a shallow one by "more convenient methods of treatment" (S. E., 1905, 7: 262–263), and allowed for "slighter, episodic cases which we see recovering under all kinds of influences and even spontaneously." And, as we recall, as part of his 1909 enunciation of NCT, he again allowed that "slight disorders may perhaps be bought to an end by the subject's unaided efforts, but never a neurosis." (S. E., 1909, 10: 104). (p. 157)

In light of this evidence, one may discard all cases of spontaneous recovery mentioned above as being "slighter, episodic cases" only, and not cases of real, full-blown neuroses. If so, it is important to modify the claim that there is no case of psychoneurosis that is cured spontaneously:

> According to Freud, if N is a case of neurosis that is not a slighter, episodic disorder but a full-blown neurosis, then N cannot be cured spontaneously without some therapeutic aid.

This however, is not clear. How does one distinguish between neuroses that are slighter, episodic disorders and those that are "real" neuroses? To apply the criterion of spontaneous remission in order to make the distinction would be circular. Has Freud given any indication? We may find some indication of Freud's meaning if we complete the sentence that Grünbaum has incompletely quoted above. The complete sentence runs as follows:

> Slight disorders may perhaps be brought to an end by the subject's unaided efforts, but never a neurosis—a thing which has set itself up against the ego as an element alien to it. (Freud, 1909b, p. 104)

It is clear that Freud is distinguishing a "slight disorder" from a full-blown "neurosis". The term "neurosis" has not been used here to designate any and every psychological disorder but disorder of a special intensity and extent—the kind that "sets itself against the ego as an element alien to it". The last phrase requires some explanation. In a very literal sense, it may be understood as follows: the neurosis is such that the symptoms or symptomatic activities have reached a proportion where the ego has no control over them. The symptoms persist and affect large areas of the personality in such a way that the ego feels overwhelmed and is unable to perform its normal functions.

When a neurosis has reached this proportion, it is no longer amenable to spontaneous cure.

The following excerpt may also help in strengthening this interpretation of the use of the term "neurosis":

> The expectation that every neurotic phenomenon can be cured may, I suspect, be derived from the layman's belief that the neuroses are something quite unnecessary which have no right whatever to exist. Whereas in fact they are severe, constitutionally fixed illnesses, which rarely restrict themselves to only a few

> attacks but persist as a rule over long periods or throughout life. (Freud, 1933a, p. 153)

Thus, it is "neurosis" in this sense that is not amenable to spontaneous remission. If the above clarification is correct, then Grünbaum's claim can be finally expressed in the following way: according to Freud, if N is a case of neurosis such that the symptoms of N have reached a proportion where the ego of P has no control over them and the symptoms persist over a long period of time and affect large areas of the personality in such a way that the ego of P is unable to perform its normal functions, then the likelihood that N will be cured spontaneously is very little. This claim of Freud is used by Grünbaum as a proof of Freud's enunciation of NCT′ implying that spontaneous cure of neurosis is not possible and only psychoanalytic therapy leading to insight can cure the N.

He then cites what he considers to be counterexamples by pointing out that (i) Freud admits later that spontaneous cure of a neurosis is possible, which undermines the strength of NCT′, and (ii) Freud's claim mentioned above is false because spontaneous cures do occur. This evidence makes NCT′ false also. Grünbaum has made the following mistakes in his reasoning: Freud's claim regarding spontaneous cure would be proof of the enunciation of NCT′ if and only if Freud had claimed that a neurosis of the sort described above could be cured only by the psychoanalytic method of treatment. The second conjunct of NCT′ expresses the claim that the psychoanalytic method of treatment is uniquely therapeutic for neuroses. But what Freud is denying is the likelihood of the cure of such a neurosis without therapeutic intervention of some sort. He is not claiming that for the cure of such a neurosis, analytic treatment is a necessary condition. In fact, in the passage quoted by Grünbaum, Freud clearly mentions the following:

> To get the better of such an element another person must be brought in, and in so far as that other person can be of assistance the neurosis will be curable. (Freud, 1909b, p. 104)

It is to be clearly noted that Freud did not claim that this other person must be a psychoanalyst, only that such a person should be able to help the patient in some relevant way. I have already cited sufficient evidence that contrary to Grünbaum's assertion, Freud does not deny that a durable cure is possible by other therapeutic interventions also. Thus, the passage quoted by Grünbaum cannot be accepted as an evidence of Freud's enunciation of NCT′. Did Freud, later in life, repudiate his claim about spontaneous remission mentioned above? Repudiation of this claim by Freud is important for Grünbaum because the empirical evidence of spontaneous cure falsified NCT′.

It may be pointed out that since the passage quoted by Grünbaum cannot be accepted as a proof of Freud's enunciation of (NCT′), consideration of this point is immaterial for my purposes. However, it may well be pointed out that there is no empirical evidence that neuroses of the sort characterised above are cured spontaneously without therapeutic intervention of some sort. The single line that Grünbaum quotes as Freud's repudiation of the unlikelihood of a spontaneous cure is taken out of context and given a twisted interpretation. A thorough reading of the whole chapter would show that Grünbaum's interpretation is false.

Thus, there is sufficient textual evidence that Freud did not believe in the extremely strong conditions stated in NCT′. However, as I have stated earlier, textual evidence is subject to different interpretations and hence does not always provide conclusive evidence for the view of a philosopher. I shall strengthen this conclusion by showing that the Tally Argument is not compatible with some of the logical consequences of psychoanalytic theory; the next section will be devoted to this consideration.

Section II

Logical consequences of psychoanalysis and NCT

Grünbaum has argued vigorously that the Tally Argument is not only in accord with the general theory of Freud, but is indispensable for the explanatory structure of the psychoanalytic theory. Contrary to Grünbaum's assertion, I shall show that the Tally Argument, especially the Necessary Condition Thesis (NCT), is not compatible with some of the logical consequences of the psychoanalytic theory. In order to do so, it will be necessary to explain the psychoanalytic mechanism of symptom formation and derive therapeutic implications from it. A neurotic symptom is a compromise-formation between the Id and the ego. Thus, a neurotic symptom is never formed due to a single factor but due to a combination of factors: the drive energy represented by the Id and *failure* of the ego to handle the demands of the Id in a realistic manner. This requires some explanation.

When a given drive energy remains undischarged due to the opposition of ego forces, it creates a state of tension in the psychic apparatus. Since the psychic apparatus is governed by the constancy principle, which states that the psychic apparatus tries to maintain a state of least tension, the ego tries to restore the equilibrium by redistribution of the psychic energy. If the redistribution leads to the satisfactory discharge of the libidinal energy, symptom formation does not take place. Usually this is achieved by successful defences like sublimation or displacement. When this cannot be achieved, the libidinal energy is repressed. We now come to important quantitative considerations, which are as follows:

(T1) The ego has to expend more and more of its available energy to maintain a counter-cathexis against the repressed impulse and thus has less and less energy to discharge its normal function. Counter-cathectic forces of the ego or forces that oppose the gratification of an instinctual impulse may roughly be characterised as the social and moral forces of the ego.

(T2) The repressed drive regresses to earlier stages of libidinal fixations and seeks gratification through activities or objects characteristic of those earlier stages.

(T3) The ego opposes these activities, since it has abandoned the pleasures of earlier phases in favour of the pleasures of the later, more mature stages.

(T4) To avoid recognition by the ego, the drive energy is manifested through strange behaviours not easily recognised as activities leading to libidinal gratification of an earlier phase of development.

(T5) The ego considers these activities as alien to itself and spends more and more energy to prevent their occurrence. This leads to suffering or serious depletion in the quota of energy that the ego requires for the performance of its normal activities or to enjoy life. Such a condition is a pathological condition.

Qualitatively speaking, according to psychoanalytical theory, there is no difference between a so-called normal person and a neurotic. The precondition of a neurosis exists in all the so-called normal people also. Falling ill or getting cured, therefore, is to be viewed as essentially a quantitative concept in psychoanalysis. It may be expressed in the following way:

> Let P be a Freudian system with a fixed quantity of drive-energy E: A neurotic symptom is the result of a distribution of psychic energy E in such a way that the ego of P is depleted in the performance of its normal activities and enjoyment of life.

From (T1)–(T5) we can derive the following therapeutic implications for the cure of neurotic symptoms:

(T6) If the ego can regain the quantity of energy sufficient for the discharge of its normal function, it will be cured.

(T7) Since the quantity of psychic energy cannot be influenced from the outside source, cure can be effected only by the redistribution of the energy already present in the psychic apparatus of P.

(T8) The redistribution essentially consists of freeing energy bound to the counter-cathectic forces of the ego of P and to the symptoms.

(T9) There are the following alternatives for obtaining the necessary psychic energy: (i) strengthen the ego to strengthen the defence against the drive; (ii) strengthen the ego to give up the defence or replace it by a more successful one; (iii) a combination of (i) and (ii).

(T9) is our road to the technique of therapy. Otto Fenichel masterfully outlines the therapeutic implications of psychoanalytic theory of neuroses. I quote:

> Since we can therapeutically influence only the ego, there are in principle only two possibilities for such influence: we can try to strengthen the ego in such a way that it more successfully carries out its defence against instinct, or we can bring the ego to give up the defence or to replace it by a more suitable one. Actually there exist combinations of these two logically contradictory methods. We can, for example, strengthen the defence against a certain instinctual impulse by providing a derivative of it with a discharge. By this partial discharge the instinct becomes relatively weaker, and the work of defence against the remainder becomes easier. (Fenichel, 1945, p. 15)

How can the ego be strengthened? There are various ways in which the ego can be strengthened; for example, by giving strong suggestions, by receiving support from authority figures, etc. These methods may strengthen the ego temporarily so that it can strengthen its defence against the drive. This is how a cure could be obtained by suggestion or supportive therapy. If the ego is strengthened enough to control the symptoms, the quantity of energy spent in the symptomatic activities is available to the ego, but the ego has still to maintain a strong defence against the offending drive. This requires maintenance of the counter-cathectic forces. Thus, the ego does not get as great a quantity of energy as it would if it did not have to maintain the defensive attitude towards the drive. This kind of cure also makes the ego dependent on the support it needs from external sources, though it is not inconceivable that in the process of maturation it may be able to correct its attitude spontaneously and the cure brought about could lead to a permanent recovery. However, if the symptoms are pervasive and involve a large part of the personality, this method often does not lead to success. We have to take recourse to alternatives (ii) or (iii) mentioned above.

In order to achieve this objective, we have to know wherein the weakness of the ego lies. We have pointed out earlier that the weakness of the ego lies in its ability to handle the Id demands in a realistic manner without taking recourse to excessive defensive measures. And why did the ego fail to do so? Psychoanalysis has the following hypotheses:

(T10) A defence against an instinct is the result of the ego's fear of the unpleasant results in the hypothetical case of the gratification of the instinct. (These unpleasant results include its own superego injunctions.)

(T11) These fears arise primarily through some of the experiences of childhood, real or imaginary, which are misinterpreted, exaggerated to an extreme degree, and projected onto the external reality.

Since symptoms appear long after such experiences have occurred, from (T10) and (T11), one could derive the following:

(T12) A part of the infantile ego with distorted perception of reality persists in the psychic apparatus of P, functions independently of the control of the mature ego, and is responsible for the symptom formation.

We are now in a position to derive the therapeutic hypothesis of psychoanalytic theory:

(T13) Subject to the limitations of the constitutional factors, cure of neurotic symptoms can be achieved if the exaggerated, imaginary and unreal perception of the reality by a part of the ego can be corrected.

The quality of the cure depends upon the degree and the extent to which this correction of the attitude of the ego can be achieved. It can be clearly noted that this hypothesis does not imply any particular method of treatment to achieve the therapeutic objective.

However, (T11) states that the distorted perception of reality is due to exaggerated real or imaginary infantile experiences. Thus, (T13) and (T11) together imply that if the appraisal of childhood experiences responsible for the distorted perception of reality by the ego can be corrected, a cure would result. This is the technique adopted by the psychoanalytic method of treatment. To achieve the therapeutic objective implied by (T13), the psychoanalytic method of treatment adopts the following therapeutic technique:

(T14) Trace the infantile experiences causally responsible for the distorted attitude of the ego and help P's mature ego to realise the imaginary and exaggerated nature of his interpretation of those experiences.

The result of a successful (T14) would lead P to have an "insight" into the causal mechanism of his symptom formation and eventually be rid of his symptoms. An "insight", therefore, can be characterised in the following way:

(T15) P has an insight into the causal mechanism of his symptom S if and only if he has traced back the pathogenic attitudes to their original childhood experiences and has recognised with appropriate and relevant emotional accompaniments the various ways in which they are affecting his present behaviour.

Let us stipulate that any therapy that does not follow a psychoanalytic method of treatment is not treating P by giving him an insight and hence is a rival therapy of psychoanalysis.

(T13) and (T11) do not rule out that the distorted perception of reality could also be corrected by some other method of treatment. The strongest assertion that (T13) and (T11) make is that (T14) is the best way to free the energy bound to the counter-cathectic forces and consequently to the symptoms. Since there are various ways to influence the functioning of the ego, it is possible to achieve the same objective by other methods of treatment in a round about way. This is what Freud has asserted in all the textual evidence I have quoted in the previous section. He was, therefore, consistent with the logical consequences of the theory.

In Grünbaum's language we can state the implication of (T11) and (T13) in the following way:

> (T11) states that exaggerated, real or imaginary infantile experiences are a necessary condition for the distorted perception of reality by the ego, and that correction of such distorted perceptions would be sufficient to bring about cure of neurotic symptoms.

NCT would be implied only if there is an additional premise: that there is only one way to correct the attitude and functioning of the ego; namely, insight into these infantile causal experiences. But the theory of psychoanalysis does not assert this additional premise. In fact, the infantile attitudes responsible for the formation of the symptoms persist in the present. The therapist has to be able to recognise those attitudes and correct them.

The process of correction is essentially a process of education and learning and can be effected in various ways. We are constantly learning and modifying our attitudes. We learn through personal experiences, we learn vicariously through the experiences of other people, we learn by finding out the causes of our behaviours, we also learn to modify our behaviour without knowing how we came to possess it in the first place. All that is needed is the correction of the distorted perception of reality. This correction of P's perception of and attitude towards reality is theoretically possible to achieve even if P is not made aware of the factors giving rise to those attitudes, though P's awareness is the best way to assure a durable therapeutic objective. The strongest claim that the theory of psychoanalytic therapy can make is that it is the best and the most effective method of treatment, but not the only one. Different degrees of therapeutic success can be achieved by various other methods of therapy, and depending upon the nature and seriousness of the disorder and insofar as they can educate the ego they will be durable also.

There are two possible objections to this interpretation: according to psychoanalytic theory, there is some quantity of psychic energy attached to the earlier childhood experiences leading to pathogenic formulations. If the quantity of this energy is large, a cure cannot be brought about without release of this energy. This necessitates the unearthing of childhood experiences without which a cure could not be effected. Thus, it is not merely the correction of the present attitudes, but also the release of the energy from early childhood experiences that is needed for cure. This leads to an assertion of NCT.

In answer to the above, it may be stated that if the pathogenic childhood experiences are such that the quantity of libido attached to those experiences is necessary for the normal functioning of the ego, then the ego could not have led a normal existence at all or could not have led a normal existence beyond the state of having those childhood experiences. This gives us a picture of serious childhood disturbance requiring immediate therapeutic intervention. However, if the child has developed into a normal adult and then has developed some neurotic symptoms, it follows that the quantity of psychic energy necessary for leading a normal life was available to the ego of P in spite of the pathogenic childhood experiences. P would be able to resume a normal life if the same quantity of psychic energy is again made available to him. In most cases of neuroses not involving great areas of personality, this energy can be made available to the ego by a modification of the faulty attitude of the ego. This modification will lead to a more realistic perception of the demand of the Id drives. Consequently, there will be a lessening of the strength of the counter-cathectic forces. The energy thus released is made available to the ego. By a fortunate combination of external factors the cure could be made durable also.

This state is not incompatible with the claim made by psychoanalytic therapy that a deeper investigation into the pathogenic attitudes of P will lead to a more assured state of permanent recovery. Psychoanalytic treatment would follow that path. Second, it may be objected that according to psychoanalytic theory of neuroses, not all pathogenic attitudes are conscious. There may be layers of defences taken by the ego to control a pathogenic attitude. Unless these defensive layers are unravelled, the pathogenic attitudes will not become conscious and thus cannot be influenced. If this is true of most of the neuroses, then the cure of neurotic disorders by rival methods of therapy that do not subscribe to the dynamic view of the mind would be virtually absent. This is practically an assertion of NCT, though it may not be an implication of the theory. Thus, Grünbaum may be right after all in attributing NCT to Freud.

An example may illustrate the objection better. Suppose, P is suffering from an obsessive thought that her child would die. Let us suppose that according to psychoanalytic theory P's unconscious hostility towards her child was first controlled by a reaction formation and resulted in an overly protective behaviour towards the child. Here, P's attitude of hostility, which is causally responsible for the formation of the symptom, is unconscious. How can a behaviour therapist who does not subscribe to a dynamic view of the mind influence this attitude and cure P of her obsession. Under these conditions, an insight becomes a necessary condition for cure. Again, Grünbaum may be right after all in ascribing NCT to Freud.

The answer to this objection is as follows: it is only insofar as the therapist is able to identify the pathogenic attitude/s and modify it/them that there will be a durable cure. If the behaviour therapist fails to identify the complex attitudes he will fail to bring about a durable cure, leading to the repeated and complicated emergence of the symptoms. This probably is the reason why behaviour therapy is more successful in cases of monosymptomatic neurotic disorders. At the present time, the data are not broad enough to justify the conclusion that a durable cure of character disorders or complex neuroses involving large areas of the personality is amenable to successful and permanent therapeutic intervention by behaviour therapy. However, it is possible that in the process of the correction of an identified attitude another unidentified problem attitude may be indirectly corrected. This unidentified attitude may be part of the complex of pathogenic attitudes. Such correction would lead to a better recovery of P. Any assessment of therapeutic success should take this factor into account.

This leads us to the conclusion that psychoanalytic theory does not imply that in no case could a cure be effected without insight into the causal mechanism of the neurotic symptoms. There are cases where a pathogenic attitude is easily identifiable and could be corrected by other methods of treatment. The implications of NCT, therefore, are not compatible with the implications of the psychoanalytic theory. The above discussion merely states in a general way the principles involved in a successful therapy. It is incumbent upon me, however, to discuss in some detail how this kind of cure could be effected by rival modes of therapy that do not treat P by giving him insight into childhood experiences and to explain how the processes involved lead to the strengthening of the ego. Since behaviour therapy has been considered as the most successful rival therapy of psychoanalysis, I shall choose its therapeutic procedures for my discussion.

Psychoanalysis and some rival therapies

The most acclaimed methods of behaviour therapy are: (i) systematic desensitisation; (ii) assertiveness training; (iii) aversive control technique and (iv) thought stopping (mostly used by Rational Emotive Therapists). There are various other methods that I shall ignore for the purposes of my discussion. I shall first give a brief description of these methods and then show how they help in strengthening the ego.

Systematic desensitisation

The fundamental thesis behind this method is that if an anxiety-producing situation is conditioned with pleasant instead of unpleasant conditions the anxiety response will be substituted by non-anxiety-producing responses. In order to achieve this objective, the method of systematic desensitisation employs the techniques of relaxation. The method is employed in the following way: the patient is asked to imagine vividly the anxiety-producing situations in increasing order of severity in different therapeutic sessions. These situations are usually related to the target symptom; for example, the phobia of snakes. The patient is taught a systematic process of muscle relaxation progressing from the lower to the upper end of the body, and is often given bio feedback instruments so that he or she can see the rate of his or her heartbeat, pulse rate, etc. In therapeutic sessions the patient is asked to imagine the least anxiety-producing situation vividly and try to relax. When the patient is successful, he or she is asked to proceed to the next item in the list of anxiety-producing situations. The process continues till the list is exhausted and the patient is considered free of symptoms. The method has been very successfully employed in cases of monophobias; it has not been successful in cases involving multiple phobias.

Assertiveness training

Contrary to first impressions, assertiveness training is not training in aggressive behaviour. As Rimm and Masters explain:

> Assertive behaviour is interpersonal behaviour involving the honest and relatively straightforward expression of feelings. Simply stated assertive training includes any therapeutic procedure aimed at increasing the client's ability to engage in such behaviour in a socially appropriate manner. Behavioural goals include the expression of negative feelings such as anger and resentment, but often assertive procedures are employed to facilitate the expression of positive feelings such as affection or praise. (Rimm & Masters, 1979, p. 81)

Training in assertive behaviour is often employed together with systematic desensitisation. Its results are often supposed to be similar to deep muscle relaxation, which has been confirmed by the reports of the patients. It is assumed to benefit the patient by: (i) producing a greater feeling of well-being and (ii) by producing greater confidence, leading to greater success in his or her social life.

Assertiveness training is employed in the technique known as psychodrama where the patient undergoes a process of emotional catharsis via the rehearsal of different imaginary role playing, which is thought to produce inhibitions.

Aversive control technique

The method of aversive control is primarily a method for (i) controlling the frequency of the occurrence of certain undesirable behaviours, and (ii) reducing the attractiveness of certain kinds of behaviour or stimuli that are responsible for eliciting them.

The techniques of the aversive control method consist mainly in introducing a negative or positive reinforcer, as the case may be, simultaneously with the occurrence of the target behaviour. A negative reinforcer includes punishment as well as withdrawal of a positive stimulus. The technique is often called counter-conditioning because:

> ... it is theoretically assumed that the original, positive, appetitive value of the stimulus was learned (conditioned); this procedure

> replaces or counters that learning by substituting the discomfort and desires for avoidance that accompany the aversive stimulus. (Rimm & Masters, 1979, pp. 354–355)

The typically aversive stimuli used in the method are electric shocks, paralysing drugs, imagining obnoxious scenes, etc. The method requires careful handling because it may lead to undesirable consequences. Also, the extinction of the target behaviour has been found to be of short duration in most cases; however, some behaviour like eating, drinking and sexual activities have been found to be easily amenable to control by aversive technique. In many cases, if an alternative positive behaviour is not substituted for the target behaviour, another undesirable behaviour, more "regressive" in nature, has been found to develop (see Rimm & Masters, 1979, p. 366).

Thought stopping

The method of thought stopping is mainly employed in Rational Emotive Therapy or RET in short, whose founder is Albert Ellis. The theoretical foundation of this therapy is that mental disorders are primarily due to a faulty thinking pattern. This thought pattern manifests itself in a chain of preconscious, implicit self-verbalisation. In therapy, RET follows the following steps: an event to which P is exposed; the chain of self-verbalisation with which P reacts to it; the emotions and behaviours arising as a consequence; and the therapist's efforts to modify the thinking pattern of P by pointing out the irrationality of such behaviour and emotions arising out of the chain of self-verbalisation to the specific event. After this process has been completed, the thought process of the patient is first disrupted by the therapist, who will ask the patient to stop the particular chain of self-verbalisation. When this is successful, the patient is instructed to give a command to him- or herself to stop the destructive chain of self-verbalisation whenever it occurs.

Summary of the four methods

If we think about these four methods outlined above, we perhaps have difficulty in differentiating them from the methods used by psychoanalysts. RET is especially close to psychoanalysis with its emphasis on introspection, discussion of feelings and emotions, and self-examination of one's irrational thought pattern leading to pathological states. However, we have to clearly bear in mind that these methods are not considered to be insight-producing, which characterises psychoanalytic therapy. These methods do not emphasise the historical past of P, and do not trace the root of the symptoms to the childhood experiences of P as is done in psychoanalytic therapy.

The method of assertive training emphasises catharsis. A variant of the method, psychodrama, often successfully brings about the emotional catharsis of deeply rooted childhood events charged with strong emotions. An acquaintance of the present author who participated in psychodrama successfully brought up intense emotions related to the death of her father in World War II. She was still a child when her father died in the war and she was unable to bring up the emotions related to the traumatic situation.

Assertiveness training begins first by finding out what kind of emotions the patient might be experiencing. A probe is then made in to whether the patient realises and accepts the existence of such emotions. If not, the therapist takes measures to convince the patient that he or she does experience those emotions. Only after this task is achieved is the patient slowly encouraged to give expression to his or her emotions in a constructive way. I quote:

> Frequently, the therapist must deal with persons whose anxiety is related to the expression of anger. Often the anxiety leads to an almost total suppression of direct expressions of hostility in the target interchange, although sometimes the individual may express anger in an ambivalent or apologetic fashion, producing unsatisfying and ineffectual performance … Once the therapist has gathered sufficient evidence that unexpressed hostility is a problem his next task is to convince the client of this, which is no minor undertaking. … We recommend that feelings of trust and confidence be first established and that the subject of the client's hostile feelings be dealt with in a graduated fashion. (Rimm & Masters, 1979, pp. 87–88)

If the book from which I have quoted the above passage were not titled *Behavior Therapy*, I could have interpreted this passage as an example of psychoanalytic writing. Success in the application of this method depends upon the therapist's ability to assess how certain behaviours lead to the non-fulfilment of some of P's desires. The behaviourist does not use this terminology, but this is essentially what he or she is doing. The behaviourist finds out the specific areas of need, the unexpressed emotion of fear or anger or anxiety, convinces the patient of its pathological role, and trains the individual in giving them proper expression. By role playing and rehearsing, P is able to overcome some of the unrealistic nature of his or her anxiety and is better able to cope with the anxiety-provoking situations.

Though all these procedures have been labelled behaviouristic, they do not eliminate the factor of a conscious, thinking agent who is correcting his or her infantile attitudes related to particular situations. In all behaviouristic approaches, there is an ineliminable uncontrolled variable; namely, a conscious agency that learns and unlearns. Thus, success of assertiveness training may be explained by pointing out that through a cathartic process part of the dammed-up energy is released, making the ego more capable of controlling the remaining state of affairs. In role playing the ego of P is confronting a situation that is similar to the one anticipated as anxiety-producing by the ego of P. By a repeated exposure to such situations, the ego may be able to realise that the anxiety that it had associated with such situations is largely imaginary. In fact, psychoanalysts proceed in a similar way in their therapeutic session. What they try to bring about by making P imagine, is brought about here by making him or her confront a situation that is similar to the one thought to be disastrous by P. Behaviourists might be surprised that long ago Freud recommended the following therapeutic procedure:

> Take the example of agoraphobia; there are two cases of it, one mild, and the other severe. Patients belonging to the first suffer from anxiety when they go into the street by themselves, but they have not given up going out alone on that account; the others protect themselves from the anxiety by altogether ceasing to go about alone. With these last one succeeds only when one can induce them by the influence of analysis to behave like the phobic patients of the first class—that is, to go into the street and to struggle with their anxiety while they make the attempt. (Freud, 1919a, p. 166)

The rationale behind the recommendation is that while forced to face the situation again and again, the ego will be able to realise the imaginary nature of its anxiety. This may help the patient in gaining control over his anxiety even without knowing the causal factors behind it.

However, psychoanalytic therapy will not stop there. It will go beyond this stage and will try to discover the experiences leading to the infantile reaction pattern. But the processes described above and used by behaviour therapy lead to the successful termination of the symptom because they achieve the following two factors: (1) the release of some dammed-up psychic energy through emotional catharsis; and (2) the repeated exposure to anxiety-producing situations leading to the correction of the infantile anxiety of the patient. Both factors lead to the strengthening of the ego and restore its ability to control the offending impulse either by strengthening the defence or by trying to fulfil it in reality. It is possible, for example, that by repeated role playing P is able to face his mother and get her permission to marry the girl he desires or to defy her. This leads to a direct satisfaction of strong libidinal desires and can bring about a permanent cure. The satisfaction obtained through social success also often provides opportunities for libidinal satisfaction and, provided P can take advantage of such a situation, may lead to the release of dammed-up psychic energy.

Both Grünbaum and Edward Erwin will have strong objections to my explanation. But here is some empirical evidence in support of my explanation. Peter Fonagy writes:

> There is even tentative evidence from the reanalysis of therapy tapes from the National Institute of Mental Health's Treatment of Depression Collaborative Research Program that the more features the process of a brief therapy (e.g. cognitive behavior therapy, interpersonal therapy) shares with that of a psychodynamic approach, the more likely it is to be effective. (Fonagy, 2000, p. 621)

There is no need for psychoanalysis to account for the success of behaviour therapy by a theory of "ghost symptoms". The success is perfectly compatible with the logical consequences of the theory. In so far as any of the above techniques employed by a therapy will be able to help P in correcting his or her irrational and infantile attitude towards certain situations, and/or help in the release of the dammed-up psychic energy, they would be strengthening the ego, which may lead to the successful termination of the problem behaviour.

It may be objected that according to psychoanalytic theory such cures should lead to symptom substitution, which is not supported by empirical evidence in these cases. It may be answered that symptom substitution would result if the attitude of the ego is not corrected as is the case in direct prohibitive suggestions. In behaviour therapy, the aversion control technique is one method that fails to effect any correction of attitude on the part of the ego of P. Occurrences similar to symptom substitution have been found to occur in those cases. However, psychoanalysts would still claim that, in general, the therapeutic gain by proper psychoanalytic treatment would be longer lasting, more encompassing and qualitatively superior to these forms of therapy. The database to date is not sufficiently broad based to refute this claim.

I have shown that according to the theory of psychoanalytic therapy, cure could be brought about in two ways: (i) either by strengthening the ego to strengthen the defence, or (ii) by strengthening the ego to give up the defence or replace it with a more suitable one. While psychoanalysis follows the second alternative, it admits that under suitable circumstances a durable cure can be achieved by employing the first alternative also or a combination of the two in different degrees; the rival therapies mostly use a combination. They identify a pathogenic attitude, help P in correcting it, or sometimes effect catharsis of repressed emotions by bringing about a situation more conducive to the release of dammed-up psychic energy. They differ from psychoanalysis only insofar as they do not trace the causal factors responsible for the development of pathogenic symptoms. This limitation still leaves room for the theory that cures brought about by psychoanalytic therapy are qualitatively superior to those of other therapies, especially in complex neurotic disorders.

In light of the above, how can Grünbaum ascribe NCT to Freud? I have extensively quoted Freud in the previous section, showing how textual evidence contradicts Grünbaum's attribution of NCT to Freud. Now I have shown that it is also incompatible with the logical consequences of the theory. However, one more point needs clarification in this context. Grünbaum has argued that NCT is indispensable for Freud in order to explain the following:

- The difference in success between the cathartic method of Breuer and his own method of free association; and
- to explain symptom substitution.

Both of these points can be explained by appeal to what Freud called "resolution of the resistance of P". The cathartic method employed the method of hypnosis, which provided no opportunity to the therapist to help P overcome his resistance. In other words, the therapist has no opportunity to either identify or to correct the infantile pathological attitudes of P. As I have discussed above, the most important factor leading to a cure is the modification of the pathogenic attitudes of the ego. The ego has to learn that some of its reactions are faulty and give them up. As I have explained above, these attitudes can be modified to some extent without knowing what caused them. But the cathartic method used under hypnosis did not provide any such opportunity, while the method of free association did. In the method of free association, resistance manifests itself constantly, thus providing an opportunity to the therapist to deal with it. This results in a continuous correction of the resisting forces of the ego. Such an opportunity is absent in treatment done under hypnosis—at least in hypnotic therapy as it was practised during Freud's time. This will explain the objections raised by Grünbaum.

Finally, I will digress a little at this point to answer one of the objections Grünbaum has raised. He cites a passage from Freud in which Freud said that only a physico-chemical therapy is a true causal therapy and interprets the passage as Freud's denial that analytic treatment is causal treatment. He chastises analysts who characterise their therapy as such. To be sure, Freud does not deny that analysis is a causal therapy but that it is not a causal therapy in the same sense in which the change in the constitutional factor is. The full passage quoted in proper context will make the point clearer:

> Well, then, is our psychoanalytic method a causal therapy or not? The reply is not a simple one ... In so far as psycho-analytic therapy does not make it its first task to remove the symptoms, it is behaving like a causal therapy. In another respect, you may say, it is not ... Supposing, now that it was possible, by some chemical means, perhaps to interfere in this mechanism, to increase or diminish the quantity of libido present at a given time or to strengthen one instinct at the cost of another—this then would be a causal therapy in the true sense of the word, for which our analysis would have carried out the indispensable preliminary work of reconnaissance. (Freud, 1916–1917, p. 436)

The confusion results due to our use of the word "cause" to designate conditions bringing about a given effect at different levels. The confusion is prevalent even today in fields other than psychoanalysis. In the field of epidemiology it is reported that:

> Even the causal frame of reference where the typhoid bacillus is regarded as the cause of typhoid fever might be open to criticism. From a molecular biology viewpoint, the typhoid bacillus can be considered the vehicle of a specific biochemical agent, which is the "true" cause of the disease.
>
> ...
>
> In fact, even if knowledge of causative agents at a molecular level were complete, it would still be necessary, in most instances, to have information on the transmitting vehicles in order to apply the measure required for the prevention and control of many diseases. Thus, it is necessary to know that polluted water is a cause of typhoid fever; the knowledge that protein "X" in the typhoid bacillus is the causative agent at the molecular level does not directly suggest the method of control. (Lilienfeld & Lilienfeld, 1980, p. 294)

This passage indicates that it is common practice to use the word "cause" to designate causal agents operating at different levels. We all know that the typhoid bacillus is the cause of typhoid fever. But at the molecular level it is the presence of a specific biochemical agent that is the cause of the typhoid fever. The typhoid bacillus is merely a carrier of this biochemical agent. Thus, a "true" causal therapy of typhoid will be the one that takes care of the specific biochemical agent, not the therapy that destroys the typhoid bacilli present in the body. But the latter also is considered a form of causal therapy, especially so because it helps in the prevention of the disease.

If such usages are accepted in the field of epidemiology, I do not see any reason why psychoanalysts should be censored for a similar use of the term "cause". Analytic therapy is a causal therapy in the sense in which the treatment of typhoid fever by destroying the typhoid bacilli is a causal therapy. The change in the constitutional factors is causal in the same sense in which the control of the biochemical agent X responsible for typhoid fever is a causal therapy. There is no discrepancy here.

If the Tally Argument does not represent Freud's position, what then is his argument? I shall present my formulation of Freud's argument in the next chapter.

CHAPTER FOUR

The problem of error

Section I

Understanding suggestibility

I promised to present my own formulation of Freud's argument in this chapter. Before taking up this task it is important to clarify two points: (i) what does the suggestibility charge entail? And (ii) what is the sense in which the term "suggestion" has been used by Grünbaum in relation to the suggestibility charge? The suggestibility charge is obviously relevant to the confirmatory status of psychoanalytic hypotheses. There are two possible ways in which it can be interpreted:

(1) In the process of psychoanalytic psychotherapy, P undergoes a strong state of suggestibility. This state of suggestibility is deliberately exploited by a psychoanalyst to elicit false data relevant for the confirmation of his or her hypotheses.
(2) In the process of psychoanalytic psychotherapy, P undergoes a strong state of suggestibility. The psychoanalytic treatment of giving an interpretation is such that this state of suggestibility would often lead to contaminated responses from P and thus to spurious confirmation of psychoanalytic hypotheses.

The first point is obviously of no concern to philosophy of science. This charge is based upon the consideration of personal integrity of a given analyst. The charge can be easily answered by pointing out that any method is subject to abuse by investigators in a given area. This is not an indication of methodological defect in the discipline concerned. Nor does it imply that genuine confirmation of the theory would not be found if the method is employed in the proper manner. Instances of deliberate falsification of data in branches of physical science or astronomy are not rare. But philosophy of science is not concerned with such cases. Grünbaum certainly wants to make a different claim. It is, therefore, the second point that refers to methodological considerations that he must have in mind. A strong state of suggestibility is an inevitable stage in the process of psychoanalytic treatment. Giving interpretations is the technique of treatment. Under such circumstances, even a proper application of the therapeutic method may increase the probability of contaminated responses on the part of P. Therefore, the suggestibility charge does not depend on the personal factors of any given analyst, but on methodological consideration.[1] In our future reference to the suggestibility charge, we shall understand it in this sense.

Since the word "suggestion" has been used in various senses, it is important to distinguish the sense that is relevant to the suggestibility charge. Webster's 9th New Collegiate Dictionary gives the following meanings for the word "suggestion":

1 a: the act or process of suggesting b: something suggested
2 a: the process by which one thought leads to another esp. through association of ideas b: a means or process of influencing attitudes and behaviour hypnotically 3: a slight indication; Trace <a—of a smile>.

Relevant for our purposes is the meaning "process of influencing attitudes and behaviour hypnotically". Though hypnosis is not used in psychoanalysis, the first part of the meaning is key for the charge of suggestibility against psychoanalysis. But this does not help us much. Not every means of influencing our behaviour or attitude is due to suggestion. One's attitude may be influenced by good reasoning, by anticipation of consequences, by foreknowledge of certain situations, by coercion, and so on. In none of these cases do we say that the person has been "suggested". Obviously there is a strong emotive connotation involved in the meaning of the word "suggestion", indicating something that a person P was made to do/think and would not have done/thought it if he or she had used critical judgement. Also, not everything that influences P's attitude and behaviour is detrimental to the validity of the data. We are constantly making suggestions to our friends and are receiving suggestions from our instructors without affecting the validity of data obtained through the means of a suggested act.

Consider the following sentences uttered by the speaker to P where the speaker is a famous biology teacher and P is his or her student: if you carefully look through the microscope you will see some round-shaped figures. Let us stipulate that there are no round-shaped figures on the slide. Now consider the following cases:

(1) P is critical of the speaker and does not trust him or her; P refuses to act as suggested.
(2) P has a high opinion of the speaker's ability and sees through the microscope with the expectation of seeing the round-shaped figures on the slide but fails to see any.
(3) P is devoted to the speaker and acts according to the suggestion. P, in fact, reports perceiving round-shaped figures on the slide.

Let us stipulate that P is in a normal state of mind, he is saying what he believes to be true in each case and his sense organs are in perfect functioning order. The first point is not a case of suggestion at all. The speaker failed to make P act according to the instruction. The second point is a case of suggestion because it influenced the attitude of P; it aroused strong expectation for some definite results to be obtained. But the influence was not strong enough to make him falsify the objective reality. The third point represents a case where the degree of influence on P was so great that the objective reality was falsified without any conscious intent on the part of P. This is the case relevant to the suggestibility charge against psychoanalysis.

The characteristic features of such a state are:

- The suggestion is given by an authority figure A or by someone whom P accepts as an authority figure.
- P is in a heightened state of readiness to accept, believe, obey or respond in the manner communicated to P by A.
- P does not have a critical attitude towards A.

Let us call this form of suggestion S_2 and distinguish it from the friendly suggestion of the instructor/friend (S_1) and from a prevalent critical attitude resulting in a negative response to any form of communication (S_0). This distinction is not an exhaustive one, nor is it supposed to be a definition of the word "suggestion". The distinction has been made to underscore the importance of the strong sense in which suggestion is relevant for the suggestibility charge. S_2 alone is a situation in which data can be contaminated by the suggestion of an analyst. Suggestion in the form of S_0 and S_1 are almost constant features of our daily communication without detriment to the objectivity of data. In fact, the suggestion of an instructor/friend may be a helpful guide in obtaining specific results. There is nothing harmful in this practice so long as it does not distort the results obtained. It may save valuable time and energy involved in innumerable trials and errors. It is in this sense that psychoanalysis claims to operate. The suggestibility charge against psychoanalysis acquires significance only if we understand "suggestion" in the sense of S_2. How does the problem arise?

The difference in the results of the three types of suggestion reflects the degree of suggestibility of P towards the person giving the suggestion. It is this degree of suggestibility of P towards A that determines whether the response of P will be of the type S_0, S_1 or S_2. The possibility of a distorted response increases with the degree of suggestibility of P towards A. The state of suggestibility of P towards A may differ in degree at different times. We have discussed above that P's response would contaminate the data only if A is able to elicit a response from P in the sense of S_2. This requires a very high degree of suggestibility of P towards A.

In the example illustrated above, we could distinguish between S_1 and S_2 because we knew what the reality was. We knew that there were no round-shaped figures on the slide. In the case of analytic therapy, we do not know what is real regarding the psychological states of P. Given this situation, the possibility of contamination arises in the following way: during the period of analysis, P is in a state of strong suggestibility towards the analyst. This is sufficient to entertain the *possibility* that P responds to the therapist's suggestion in the sense of S_2. If analytic therapy uses suggestion in the sense of S_1, the burden of proof is on the therapist to prove that the clinical data are not contaminated. If a cure of neurotic symptoms is obtained by analytic therapy, it is for the analyst to prove that P's response is not determined by the suggestion of the therapist in the sense of S_2, but is due to insight.

It is this proof that Freud is engaged in supplying in his "Analytic therapy" lecture. Thus, Freud is trying to reply to the following specific charge: since during analytic therapy P passes through a state of strong suggestibility, it is possible that the cure obtained was due to the suggestion in the sense of S_2, and not due to insight as claimed by analysts. Freud's task is to refute this and show that the interpretations given to P during his state of suggestibility acted as suggestions only in the sense of S_1. In analytic therapy, the state of transference is characterised as the state of strong suggestibility of the patient towards his or her analyst. This is an inevitable part of the therapy and is the source of the objection Freud is trying to reply to. Thus, given the method of analytic treatment, there is only one way in which the above charge can be refuted; namely, by appealing to a characteristic of cure that suggestion is insufficient to bring about. This is the principal strategy that Freud has adopted in his "Analytic therapy" lecture. I shall present my formulation of Freud's argument below.

The insufficiency theses

Freud's argument as to what the suggestibility charge entails is based upon two major characteristics that S_2 is insufficient to bring about. I shall call them The Insufficiency Thesis (1) (henceforth referred to as IT.1) and The Insufficiency Thesis (2) (henceforth referred to as IT.2). IT.1 may serve as a criterion for judging the therapeutic results of analytical treatment while IT.2 may serve as a criterion for judging whether the data produced in the treatment sessions are contaminated by the suggestion of the analyst or not. These two distinct criteria should serve to validate the theoretical and the therapeutic claims of psychoanalysis separately.

According to Freud, the theoretical validity of psychoanalytic hypotheses is not dependent upon their therapeutic success or failure. The clinical data consist of everything that the patient says or does in the clinical session. If these data are valid, they may confirm or disconfirm a given psychoanalytic hypothesis under investigation independently of the success or failure of the therapeutic process. This is abundantly clear from the following passage in the same "Analytic therapy" lecture on which Grünbaum has based his Tally Argument:

> Nor must we fail to point out that a large number of the individual findings of analysis, which might otherwise be suspected of being products of suggestion, are confirmed from another and irreproachable source. Our guarantors in this case are the sufferers from dementia praecox and paranoia, who are of course far above any suspicion of being influenced by suggestion. (Freud, 1916–1917, p. 453)

The above passage is a clear indication that Freud is not basing his argument on the therapeutic success of psychoanalysis. In spite of Freud's repeated assertions, Grünbaum ignores this point and claims that this is merely a kind of salesmanship on the part of Freud (see *Foundations*, p. 141). I shall illustrate below both the insufficiency theses.

Insufficiency Thesis 1 (IT.1)

The major premise of Freud's argument comes from his own experience of purely suggestive therapies. His experience in hypnotic therapy led him to conclude that the results of suggestive therapy are capricious, impermanent, and require a state of maintained dependence on the part of the patient towards the therapist. The cure obtained through S_2 is coexistent with the state of suggestibility of P towards his therapist. He begins his "Analytic therapy" lecture by saying:

> I practiced hypnotic treatment for many years ... I can therefore speak of the results of hypnotic or suggestive therapy on the basis of a wide experience ... The procedure was not reliable in any respects. ... Worse than the capriciousness of the procedure was the lack of permanence in its successes. If after a time, one has news of the patient once more, the old ailment was back again or its place had been taken by a new one. (Freud, 1916–1917, p. 449)

Long before he wrote the above passage, he had said the same thing in 1905:

> I gave up suggestive technique, and with it hypnosis, so early in my practice because I despaired of making suggestion powerful

> and enduring enough to effect permanent cures. In every severe case I saw the suggestions which had been applied crumble away again; after which the disease or some substitute for it was back once more. (Freud, 1905a, p. 261)

On the basis of this empirical evidence, he formulates the first premise of his argument by appealing to the insufficiency of S_2 to bring about a cure beyond the state of suggestibility of P. This insufficiency of suggestion may be expressed in the following way:

(IT.1) By and large S_2 is insufficient to bring about a cure that lasts beyond the state of suggestibility of P towards his therapist.

In my opinion, this forms one of the premises of Freud's argument in his "Analytic therapy" lecture—an important premise that Grünbaum has neglected to mention and that is responsible for his mistaken formulation of Freud's argument. In fact, the scope of IT.1 may be considered to be broader than a mere defence of a psychoanalytic method of treatment. It may be interpreted as a *test* of therapeutic gain by *any form of therapy*. If the results of a treatment outlast the period of suggestibility of the patient towards his therapist, then the results are not due to suggestion. This may be construed as a general test for any method of treatment that may have to face the charge of suggestibility.

Once it is decided whether the results are due to suggestion or not, one can venture to find out what specific features of the therapy in question were responsible for the therapeutic gain. For example, it may be claimed that the therapeutic gain of behaviour therapy is a placebo effect and is the result of the relationship between the therapist and the patient. Freud would ask to apply IT.1. Do the results of the therapy outlast the influence of the therapist on the patient? Is the favourable outcome of the treatment maintained even after the favourable relationship between the therapist and the patient has run its course? If so, the results are not due to suggestion. Once this question is settled it would then be a matter of theoretical investigation to find out which or what specific features of the treatment process contributed to the therapeutic gain.

That IT.1 is the basis of Freud's argument against suggestibility in the sense of S_2 is evident from the following passage:

> We look upon successes that set in too soon as obstacles rather than as a help to the work of analysis; and we put an end to such

> successes by constantly resolving the transference on which they are based. It is this last characteristic which is the fundamental distinction between analytic and purely suggestive therapy, and which frees the results of analysis from the suspicion of being successes due to suggestion … At the end of an analytic treatment the transference must itself be cleared away; and if success is then obtained or continues, it rests, not on suggestion, but on the achievement by its means of an overcoming of internal resistances, on the internal change that has been brought about in the patient. (Freud, 1916–1917, p. 453)

It is clear from the above passage that if the therapeutic gains do not outlast the state of suggestibility of P, Freud would grant that the treatment gain was due to suggestion. Before I proceed further, it will be in order to consider one possible objection to IT.1; that it provides us with a vague criterion because of the following reasons:

(a) There is no clear-cut criterion by which one could ascertain with reasonable certainty that the state of suggestibility of P has been dissolved.
(b) In spite of the apparent independence of the patient P, P may harbour imperceptible reliance on her therapist and the continuation of the therapeutic gain could be due to such features.
(c) It is possible that causing a person to believe that he understands the cause of his behaviour somehow gives the person a sense of confidence or the feeling that he is able to change. Maybe this sort of thing frees some psychic energy and does enable a person to overcome the problem, even after the suggestibility relation has ended. Broadly speaking, this treatment gain would also be due to suggestion. If this is true, cure would outlast the state of suggestibility of P towards his therapist, but it is still due to suggestion in the sense of S_2.

In reply to (a), it may be stated that the criterion of freedom from the state of suggestibility is no vaguer than the criterion of the state of suggestibility. If a charge against a therapy is based upon the existence of a specific psychological state of the patient, then there must be some distinguishing features of the state by virtue of which it can be differentiated from other psychological states. If so, the absence of such features may be reasonably construed as the absence of the psychological state in question.

In reply to (b), it may be stated that the state of suggestibility relevant for our purpose is an exaggerated one. Mild states of suggestibility would fail to influence P to distort the data. These exaggerated states are easily distinguishable from normal states of P. The persistence of such states in mild form (in the sense of S_0 and S_1) is not relevant for our purposes. Thus, I propose the following criterion for determining whether a given person P is free from the state of suggestibility in the sense of S_2 or not:

> If P has been in a state of S_2 towards his therapist at a time t, then P is free from such a state of S_2 if, at a later time t′, P is, by and large, not experiencing and exhibiting those behavioural features that characterised him as being in a state of S_2 at t.

This criterion should not be considered an empty one, because, we do recognise whether P is in a state of suggestibility or not by observing his excessive dependence on his therapist, his uncritical acceptance of the therapist's instructions, his faith and belief in the general ability of the therapist, etc. If these features are sufficient to determine that P is in a state of suggestibility towards his therapist, then absence of these features by and large should be sufficient to pronounce him free from the state of suggestibility towards his analyst. Therefore, this is not an empty or vague criterion.

In reply to (c), this is a stronger objection and is based upon the more subtle effects of suggestion. Essentially, it is asserting that all the therapeutic interpretations given during the therapy may be false or may not be causally related to the cure of P. P may have simply developed a false belief regarding the causal factors behind his symptoms. In other words, the so-called insight may be a "pseudo insight" and the cure may actually be due to suggestion. This objection points out that Freud's IT.1 may have taken into account only the crude forms of suggestion that occur in hypnotic treatment or are manifested in the form of leading questions of the therapist. It fails to counter the effects of the subtler and indirect forms of suggestion, which may be therapeutically effective and thus are counterexamples to IT.1. I do not think that Freud has a good defence against (c). My contention is that he would probably appeal to empirical evidence related to the type of neurotic disorder concerned. For example, he might say that it is highly unlikely that a severe character disorder or a severe obsession neurosis is cured merely by the confidence generated in the patient by the utterances of the therapist.

It should be noted, however, that IT.1 merely indicates whether the therapeutic gain is due to suggestion or not. In other words, it performs an eliminative function only. In order to arrive at the actual causal factor responsible for the gain in treatment, other relevant possible factors need to be taken into account and properly eliminated as possible candidates for sufficiency to bring about the gain.

Insufficiency Thesis 2 (IT.2)

Freud provides us with another condition that in his opinion S_2 is insufficient to bring about. It is not as obvious as IT.1, but it is implied by his argument. I state it below:

(IT.2) By and large, if proper techniques of analysis are followed, suggestion is insufficient to bring about a psychological state C in P such that P seems to be emotionally reliving C with all the associated and relevant psychological processes for a prolonged period of the therapy.

The Insufficiency Thesis 2 requires some explanation. The crucial phrase here is "if proper techniques of analysis are followed". The proper therapeutic techniques of analysis require, among other things, that (i) the analyst refrain from using suggestive language as far as possible; (ii) that the analyst encourage the patient to give free expression to his or her thoughts, feelings, desires, etc. In some cases the patient is even instructed not to read analytic literature also.

The IT.2 simply claims that if suggestions are not given following the rules of analytic therapy, then it is highly unlikely that the intense emotions that P is experiencing and living through during the course of therapy are the products of suggestion. In making his claim for IT.2 Freud obviously believes in the following:

> In order to bring about intense emotion in such a way that P would appear to be reliving a past experience, strong extensive suggestion of the right kind is a necessary condition.

It is possible to induce a strong state of emotion in hypnotised subjects. In fact, such induced emotions are often used for experimental studies on emotions. Therefore, it would be false to say that a state of strong emotion that is not related to the real past experience of P cannot be brought about by suggestion. But the necessary condition associated with such emotions produced in the laboratory—namely, the hypnotised state of the subjects and the direct and powerful suggestion given to the subject by the therapist or the experimenter—is absent in the analytic situation. In the absence of these factors, when the analyst follows the proper technique of analytic therapy it is highly unlikely that P would be experiencing a state of intense emotions such that he or she appears to be reliving it, but P has never experienced it before either in reality or in phantasy. The proper techniques of the therapy include (i) never give an interpretation without having sufficient evidence about the existence of a state of mind, and (ii) never give direct suggestion.

It may be argued that IT.2 is simply false. Highly motivated subjects can reproduce almost every state in the state of hypnotism. The analysand in a therapy situation is highly motivated to please the therapist and hence may falsely reproduce the psychological state suggested by the therapist. Experimental data are not conclusive on this subject. It is doubtful whether there is no difference in a waking state of suggestibility and a state of suggestibility induced under hypnosis. There is, however, evidence that the knowledge on the part of the experimenter or the therapist that P is not hypnotised affects the therapist's behaviour towards P. The experimenter finds him- or herself unable to give suggestions to P with the same ease and command to a waking subject as he could to a hypnotised subject.

Furthermore, there is experimental evidence that if a strong emotion has been induced under hypnotic trance, P could recall that the experience was an induced one and it fails to affect his real life situation. This indicates that if the emotional experiences P relived in the analytic situation are falsely induced by the analyst's suggestion, P would be able to recall them at a later time and it would fail to affect his or her reality adjustment or bring about a change of behaviour. It is important to note that the state of dependence of P on A is not such that P is a puppet in the hands of A. These findings put a limit to what suggestion can achieve.

Freud stated time and again that he had failed to give any suggestion to his patients in such a way that the patients seemed to be emotionally reliving it. Grünbaum himself has quoted Freud on this topic:

> I have never yet succeeded in forcing on a patient a scene I was expecting to find in such a way that he seemed to be living through

> it with the appropriate feelings. (S. E., 1896, 3: 205) ... Even twenty-eight years after his repudiation of the seduction aetiology, he is unrelenting on this point; "I do not believe even now that I forced the seduction phantasies on my patients, that I 'suggested' them". (S. E., 1925, 20: 34). (*Foundations*, p. 158)

It is IT.2 that Freud appeals to when he says in "Analytic therapy":

> The doctor has no difficulty, of course, in making him a supporter of some particular theory and in thus making him share some possible error of his own. In this respect the patient is behaving, like anyone else—like a pupil—but this only affects his intelligence, not his illness. After all, his conflicts will only be successfully solved and his resistances overcome if the anticipatory ideas he is given tally with what is real in him. (Freud, 1916–1917, p. 452)

This crucial passage has been read as a circular argument of Freud by Sutherland (see *Foundations*, p. 172), and Grünbaum has based his NCT on this passage. I claim that both readings are incorrect. It is easy to read Freud's statement as circular if one fails to recognise the implied premise of IT.2. My formulation of Freud's argument below will make the point clearer. IT.2 may be taken as a test or criterion to ascertain whether the data produced by P in the therapeutic session are contaminated by the suggestion of the therapist. If a reminiscence or a narrative of a psychological state—be it fear, guilt, envy, or any other intense emotion—is recapitulated by P in such a way that P seems to be experiencing all the appropriate emotions relevant to the state being described and there is absence of explicit suggestion by the therapist, then the probability that such data are contaminated by S_2 is very low. IT.2 is implied by Freud's argument in his "Analytic therapy" lecture. What Freud is emphasising in the quoted passage is that mere intellectual knowledge is insufficient to bring about a cure. It is the emotional reliving of the relevant traumatic situations that can help the patient to get relief from his or her symptoms.

We are now ready to present Freud's argument. Since Freud is answering the suggestibility charge against the therapeutic gain of psychoanalysis, his argument assumes that there are only two rival causal candidates for the therapeutic gain obtained through psychoanalytic treatment. Given that a patient P has been cured by analytic treatment how can we establish that P has been cured by his or her insight into the causal mechanism of his or her symptom as the therapy claims and not by suggestion. Freud gives the following argument:

(1) if P has been cured by analytic treatment, then P is either cured by insight or by suggestion
(2) suppose, P is cured by suggestion;
(3) if so, the cure would last only while the state of suggestibility of P towards her therapist lasts, (by IT.1).
(4) In analytic therapy, after the analysis, the state of suggestibility (transference) of P is dissolved but the cure is maintained.
(5) Therefore, the cure is not due to suggestion but due to insight.

This argument is an amended version of what I have referred to as Freud's second argument in Chapter Two. Freud could have stopped here. The rest of the argument is merely an explication of cure due to insight. The claim that a cure has been brought about by insight is a strong claim. The steps may be considered implied by (5):

(1) For any cure by insight, it is a necessary condition for P to overcome his resistances and resolve his conflicts.
(2) Overcoming resistances and the resolution of conflict is not possible without emotionally reliving them;
(3) therefore, if cure is due to insight, P must have emotionally relived his conflicts and resistances, guided by the interpretations of the therapist.
(4) The interpretations leading to such resolutions are insufficient to induce false emotional reliving of relevant psychological states because they were given by following the proper techniques of psychoanalysis;
(5) therefore, the probability is low that the relevant data in the clinical sessions confirming the interpretations are false.

This formulation is free from circularity. Yet it is surprising that Sutherland did not see the implied IT.2. It becomes clear if we read the passage in question together with the following passages:

> These accusations are contradicted more easily by an appeal to experience than by the help of theory. Anyone who has himself carried out psycho-analyses will have been able to convince himself on countless occasions that it is impossible to make suggestions to a patient in *that way*. (my emphasis) (Freud, 1916–1917, p. 452)

The last sentence expresses the Insufficiency Thesis (2). The phrase *that way* is rendered meaningful only if we interpret it as "the way in which P would be emotionally reliving such experiences" without which his or her conflicts and resistances would not be resolved. Thus, Freud is saying in the previous paragraph that it is not possible for the analyst to suggest anything to P in such a way that he would be emotionally reliving them given the techniques of analytic therapy. Suggestion can affect only the intelligence of P, but that is insufficient to affect his illness in most cases. Thus, he continues:

> The doctor has no difficulty, of course, in making him a supporter of some particular theory and in thus making him share some possible error of his own. In this respect the patient is behaving, like anyone else—like a pupil—but this only affects his intelligence, not his illness. After all, his conflicts will only be successfully solved and his resistances overcome if the anticipatory ideas he is given tally with what is real in him. (Freud, 1916–1917, p. 452)

If the interpretation given to the patient by his analyst were false, the analyst would have failed to bring about the emotional reliving and thus the cure. Obviously Sutherland has read it in the following way:

> If a cure has occurred by psychoanalytic treatment, then it must have occurred by insight and not by suggestion, because the conflicts of P cannot be resolved by an interpretation that does not tally with what is real in P.

This reading is circular. But this is not Freud's argument. Freud is emphasising that, first, one must eliminate suggestion as a possible candidate for cure by applying IT.1. Since there are only two possible candidates for therapeutic gain, the elimination of suggestion leads us to the hypothesis that the cure must be due to insight. If so, the interpretations must have been true, because of IT.2. Without this formulation, one cannot make sense of Freud's argument. One would either give it a circular reading as Sutherland has done or would ascribe an extremely strong condition like NCT to Freud as Grünbaum has done.

However, there is another charge of circularity that I must answer. As I have stated in Chapter Two, Grünbaum also raises a charge of circularity against Freud. This charge is essentially directed against Freud's contention that "At the end of an analytic treatment the transference must itself be cleared away; and if success is then obtained or continues, it rests, not on suggestion, but on the achievement by its means of an overcoming of internal resistances, on the internal change that has been brought about in the patient" (Freud, 1916–1917, p. 453). This has been formulated as a separate argument by Grünbaum and rejected as being viciously circular.

The claim that the transference of P, which is the state of suggestibility of P, is dissolved at the end of the treatment and the cure outlasts the state of suggestibility has been objected to by Grünbaum in the following way:

> Resolution of the transference is achieved by convincing the patient of the real origin of his transference attitude; namely, of his earliest object attachment during the repressed period of his childhood.

The above is based on two theoretical hypotheses:

(i) Transference is the product of the earliest object attachment during the repressed period of childhood.
(ii) This transference is resolved by the patient's gaining insight into the causal mechanism of transference.

Justification of the transference hypothesis is obtained from the clinical data. But the clinical data are supposed to be contaminated from the very beginning. How could we, therefore, know that the transference is dissolved? Grünbaum says that the validation of the hypotheses is viciously circular. In reply to this objection, it may be stated that to rebut the suggestibility charge validation of the transference hypothesis is irrelevant. It is sufficient for Freud to show that the success of the treatment is maintained even after the state of suggestibility is over. We simply need to know whether the characteristic behaviours or attitude that characterised a state of P as a state of suggestibility are maintained with the same intensity after the cessation of the treatment. If not, we can consider P free from the state of suggestibility. In order to do this, validation of the transference hypothesis is immaterial and irrelevant. Even extra-clinical reports of P's behaviour can perform this function. Validation of the transference hypothesis is important for the theory of psychoanalysis, not to rebut the suggestibility charge. Thus, whether P is free from his state of suggestibility towards his analyst or not can be judged by independent behavioural criterion, as I have pointed out. It is not dependent on the validation of the transference hypothesis. Grünbaum's objection is misdirected.

The basic point of difference between Grünbaum's formulation of Freud's argument and my formulation of Freud's argument is as follows: according to Grünbaum's Tally Argument, if a cure has occurred in the course of psychoanalytic treatment, it must be due to insight. This is a logical consequence of NCT, as we have pointed out before. According to my formulation, if a cure has occurred during the course of treatment, the analyst cannot immediately be certain whether the cure is due to insight or due to suggestion. The analyst has to eliminate the factor of suggestion as a possible candidate for cure. Only when the factor of suggestion is ruled out as a possible candidate for cure can the analyst conclude that the cure is due to insight. (I am assuming that these two are the only causal factors.) Therefore, according to my formulation of Freud's argument, insight is a sufficient condition for cure, not a necessary condition.

According to Grünbaum's formulation, insight is the only way for the cure of a psychoneurotic disorder. According to my formulation, Freud is claiming that insight is the best and the most efficacious way for the cure of a psychoneurosis. Grünbaum has reconstructed Freud's argument in deterministic terms. My formulation is in probabilistic terms. If Freud accepts that positive therapeutic gains could be achieved by therapeutic means other than psychoanalysis (as I have taken pains to show), his argument cannot be formulated in deterministic terms as Grünbaum has done.

I do not think that Freud was asserting as strong a thesis as Grünbaum has ascribed to him. It is highly unlikely that Freud would be ignorant of the cases of spontaneous remission and the role of environmental factors in the cure of neuroses, which is indicated by the text I have quoted. Hence, I conclude that Grünbaum's reconstruction of Freud's argument is unacceptable. However, this does not answer the suggestibility charge against psychoanalysis. We are confronted with the question as to whether my formulation of Freud's argument answers the suggestibility charge. Does it satisfactorily perform the dual role for which it was formulated? If not, is there any other way to answer the suggestibility charge?

Section II

Sources of error

It is obvious that the tenability of this argument depends on the soundness of the two Insufficiency Theses. Insofar as there is empirical support for these, the argument is rendered more probable. Freud's own experience regarding the therapeutic effect of suggestion provides some strong but limited support to IT.1. His personal experience with hypnosis led him to reject it as an unreliable therapeutic method. There is sufficient evidence to support IT.1 so far as direct, authoritarian suggestion is concerned. But this support is a limited support only. It takes into account only the crudest form of suggestion. Modern research has indicated that emotions brought about by suggestion in laboratories have later been recalled as "suggested" and had no influence on the real life of the subject (Fromm & Shore, 1979). This provides very strong support for both IT.1 and IT.2.

A great deal of sophistication has been introduced in hypnotherapy since Freud's time. Today hypnotherapy is rarely practised in isolation. It has been modified to incorporate some of the major therapeutic techniques of other forms of psychotherapy—psychoanalysis, behaviour therapy or cognitive therapy, etc. Furthermore authoritative suggestion has given way to more sophisticated, subtle suggestion. Does Freud's argument take into account this subtle form of suggestion? It is not clear that it does. Is there sufficient empirical support for Insufficiency Thesis (1) regarding this subtle form of influence also? I am tempted to answer in the affirmative but I am unable to produce empirical evidence for my claim. It may be objected to against IT.1 that even if one accepts that the therapeutic gains of direct suggestion last only while the state of suggestion of P lasts, it is conceivable that suggestion given in subtle and indirect ways may produce therapeutic gains that last even after P's state of suggestibility is over. On the basis of this, it may be claimed that Freud's inference that cure is due to insight is not justified according to the cannons of eliminative induction. A rival candidate for therapeutic gain remains uneliminated. The argument fails to save psychoanalysis from the suggestibility charge.

This objection is difficult to counter given the present simple form of the argument. In fact, my own belief is that Freud was simply trying to defend the therapy. He did it mostly by appealing to IT.1. The rest follows as a logical consequence of the conclusion he arrived at.

But Freud's argument is too simple and weak. It cannot be successfully employed to defend psychoanalysis against the suggestibility charge in all its forms. However, one may wonder whether it is really necessary for Freud to defend the theory with the help of the therapy. If a given therapeutic hypothesis is entailed by an aetiological hypothesis, the validation of the former will provide evidential support for the latter. But the results of the therapy must be shown to be causally related to the therapy in question. So long as such evidence is not available, success or failure of the therapy will have little evidential value for the validation of the theory. Given these limitations, independent evidence for the reliability of the data is a better alternative than to appeal to the success of the therapy.

If the above observation is correct, then Freud's approach is wrong. He need not appeal to the success of the therapy to counter the suggestibility charge. A weaker argument showing why the data are considered sufficiently reliable should be able to perform the task. The validation of psychoanalytic theory need not be dependent on its therapeutic success or failure. The suggestibility charge is essentially related to the prevalence of error in the data produced in the clinical setting. Unreliability of data may affect theory validation in two ways: (a) by helping to validate a hypothesis when it is false; and (b) by helping to falsify a hypothesis when it is true. To avoid these two erroneous conclusions, experimental settings attempt to control all known sources of error that may affect the test situation. Observations made under experimental situations are considered more reliable because of this reason. If the testing area is the clinical setting, and confirmatory evidence is coming from the clinical data, it is important that all known sources of error that may affect the reliability of the data are controlled.

According to the traditional concept of theory validation, any claim for the reliability of the data must fulfil two conditions:

(i) All known sources of error in the data have been controlled.
(ii) The extent of bias in the data or in the testing situation due to uncontrolled sources of error should be identified and appropriate statistical measures should be adopted to counter the bias.

However, the first condition is often difficult to satisfy. In an experimental testing of a hypothesis, three kinds of variables are important. Whose change of behaviour we are studying in a given experiment is the dependent variable. The variable that may explain the changes in the dependent variable is the independent variable, often called the experimental variable. Third, a confounding variable is one that is distributed differently in the experimental and control group and plays some role in producing the change in the dependent variable. For example, if we want to study the effect of smoking in the rate of lung cancer, the dependent variable is the rate of lung cancer, the independent variable is the rate or prevalence of smoking in the population being studied, and the confounding variable may be, say, a genetic factor G, which may be causally related in the increased rate of cancer among the smokers.

Some confounding variables can neither be controlled, nor can their effects be measured. For example, in testing the role of smoking in cancer, the confounding variable of a possible genetic factor can neither be controlled nor measured. However, in some cases confounding variables can be eliminated indirectly; for example, the confounding variable of genetic factor G in causing cancer can be eliminated indirectly. Persons who have given up smoking have been found to have a lower chance of getting cancer. This eliminates the genetic factor in cancer. The reasoning for this is the following: the genetic factor is the constant factor in the case of an individual. If this were the causally relevant factor, giving up smoking should not make any difference in such cases. But when it does make a difference, one can conclude that it was smoking rather than the genetic factor that was of causal significance.

The same is true with regards to various psychological studies. For example, the parents' disposition to allow their children to mix freely with children of all backgrounds is a confounding variable whose effect is difficult to measure. It will remain as an unmeasured confounding variable in a study, say, that tests the sociability of children in the day-care centre and in homes. In spite of the presence of such confounding variables, the results of these studies are generally accepted if the major sources of errors have been taken care of.

In light of the above discussion, we can restate the suggestibility charge against psychoanalysis in the following way: in an analytic setting neither all sources of error can be controlled nor can the extent of the bias due to these uncontrollable sources of error be identified or statistical measures be adopted to counter the bias, hence the claimed confirmation of the theory is unacceptable. As I have just pointed out, to counter this it is not necessary to appeal to the therapeutic success of analytic therapy. The IT.2 is better suited to perform this task than IT.1.

In the discussion below, I shall show that by strengthening IT.1 and IT.2, errors can be controlled and biases can be identified.

In the statistical testing of hypotheses, two sources of error are generally recognised: (i) errors due to external bias and (ii) errors due to internal bias. External bias refers to errors related to the process of sampling. Internal bias is primarily related to the control of confounding variables. Various statistical measures have been devised to control these sources of error. It is more difficult to control sources of internal bias than to control sources of external bias. In an experiment, controlling errors due to the possibility of a confounding variable is more difficult than controlling errors due to a sampling process. However, the results of an experiment are made more reliable by identifying these sources of bias and controlling them by adopting various statistical measures.

A similar approach can be taken regarding clinical data. In a clinical situation, we are mostly concerned with the problem of internal bias. In this connection, the suggestive influence of the analyst is an important confounding variable. Another source of error in the data could be the unreliability of memory of the verbal report of P in the clinical setting. Grünbaum's charge that the data are irretrievably contaminated would be true if there was no possible way either to control these sources of error or to measure their contaminating influence. But this charge is false. It is possible to control as well as to measure to a large extent the influence of contamination regarding all the above sources of error in the clinical setting. This would involve (i) identifying the sources of error and controlling them, and (ii) computing the magnitude of errors due to uncontrolled sources and dealing with them statistically.

Sources of error in clinical data

Unlike Grünbaum, I begin with the assumption that not all data in the clinical setting are contaminated. The patient has not come to the analyst with the explicit intention of telling lies about herself and others unless pathological lying is included in her symptoms. The patient is troubled and is in need of help. Her report is subject to distortion insofar as she is subject to general fallibility of memory, self-deception, and the subtle influences of the analyst. These constitute the important sources of error. Keeping the above qualifications in mind, we may classify sources of error in the clinical data into two groups: (i) non-theory-based errors, and (ii) theory-based errors. The first one will include errors not related specifically to the psychoanalytic theory or to the clinical situation. For example, errors related to memory recall of a long past event are germane to the nature of memory and not to the clinical situation itself. Errors related to the generic word "suggestion" belong to (ii). I shall first deal with the problem of memory.

The problem of memory

Grünbaum has rejected all evidence based on memory on the grounds that: (i) our memories are extremely malleable; people have pseudo memories of events that never occurred, and (ii) we have a tendency to fill up the gaps in our memories by unconscious inference. But such a drastic measure is unwarranted. Most of the memory reports can be checked for their accuracy. False and inaccurate memory reports can be isolated with a fair degree of certainty. Also, it will be better if we clarify in what sense memory reports are important for the purposes of psychoanalytic theory validation. This can best be illustrated with the help of an example; suppose the hypothesis to be tested is the following:

> The castration threat received during the oedipal period played a causal role in the neurosis of P.

Let us suppose that P does report a number of different occasions when as a child he received threats of castration. The hypothesis to be tested has three components:

(a) there exists a state having the characteristic features of what is termed oedipal phase;
(b) during this period P received castration threats; and
(c) this castration threat is causally related to P's symptoms.

P's memory reports confirm an oedipal phase and castration threats. Evidence of a different kind is required to confirm that this is related to P's symptoms, which is the causal conjunct. The question then arises as to how accurate the report has to be in order to provide evidential support to the relevant parts of the hypothesis? The answer is easy enough. All that is needed to support (a) and (b) is that such threatening situations did occur in the life of P more or less during the time period specified by the hypothesis. Thus, the most that is required of this kind of report is that it should be correct in its essence. In other words, a number of irrelevant criteria can be immediately eliminated. These are:

(1) P is required to bring up the relevant memories exactly in the order in which they occurred.
(2) P is required to bring up the relevant material in full detail correctly reporting the time, place and persons involved.
(3) If P has filled up some gaps in the reported events by her imagination, the recall loses all evidential value.

What is required is that a memory report not be false in its essential aspects. The essential aspect of a memory report is that which concerns its central theme, which has a direct bearing on the confirmation of the hypothesis. Thus, we will consider a memory report false if and only if it is false with respect to its central theme. To check whether a memory report is false essentially, the following measures can be adopted: reports from parents or other relatives can be obtained to corroborate the testimony of P. In doing so, one should look for inter-subjective agreement between the reports. Checking the internal consistency of a report is considered a good measure of the accuracy of a report. This method is often employed in controlled psychological inquiries, especially in single subject research. Freud long ago proposed this measure. Grünbaum agrees that it is a good measure for checking the validity of a memory report but then goes on to say that this does not detract from the fact that childhood memories of adult life are, in general, less reliable than the adult memories of adult life. Grünbaum's objection misses the point. It is because they are less reliable that stringent measures are needed to check their veridicality.

A general theme repeatedly appearing in the report of P under the analytic situation, even though suffering from the pitfalls of memory, is highly unlikely to be false in essence. In general, if a report is accompanied by appropriate emotions, it is less likely to be false. Grünbaum has cited the example of a false childhood memory of Jean Piaget, which was vivid and detailed but was false. Such isolated cases are not sufficient to destroy the evidential value of memory in general especially where other stringent measures are being taken to safeguard errors in the memory reports of P. Grünbaum's objection against the memory reports produced in the clinical setting seems to be based on the demand that these reports must be known to be conclusively true. If it can be inferred from the data with reasonable certainty that a given memory report is true, there is no reason to discard the data.

It may be objected that memory reports considered crucial to psychoanalysis are generally reports of emotionally charged events. It is possible that people are more apt to have faulty memories with regard to such reports. Thus, in spite of all the precautions detailed above, a psychoanalytic clinical setting may be more apt to produce false incidents of memory reports relevant to its theoretical hypotheses. However, we do not yet know whether reports of emotionally charged events are more apt to be false than reports of emotionally insignificant events. All that can be said about this objection is that a combination of internal consistency, checking the report from external sources if required, checking for the recurrence of the same theme repeatedly, and checking whether the report is accompanied by appropriate emotions should be applied whenever necessary, which is important but it is the emotional significance of the event for the patient that is of greater importance.

The problem of suggestion: theory-based error

This problem is of a more serious nature. In fact, one of the chief complaints against psychoanalytical clinical data is its unreliability due to theory-based errors. The generic charge of suggestibility is based upon a complex notion. The two main sources of error in this respect are what Paul Meehl (1983) has termed content implantation and selective intervention. The first source of error is related to the suggestive influence of the therapist. It is alleged that memories, thoughts and even defences can be explicitly "taught" to the patient. The second is biased evidence sifting. The analyst's technical decision to selectively intervene may induce a selective reinforcement of specific types of responses in P. Thus, the evidence that emerges in the clinical setting is biased. It is to be noted that it need not necessarily be false. It is in this connection that we can apply certain measures in the clinical setting, taking cue from IT2.

Freud's IT.2 states that if proper techniques are applied in analytic sessions content implantation can be controlled to a large extent. If so, then specific psychological states like emotional reliving, which by virtue of their nature are difficult to induce by indirect suggestion, are indications for the reliability of clinical data. IT.2 can be strengthened by the following considerations: if the charge of content implantation is true, it indicates that (i) P is in a strong state of suggestibility towards his therapist; and (ii) the therapist does give suggestion to P directly or indirectly.

Since (i) and (ii) are jointly necessary and sufficient conditions for the suggestive influence of the analyst to operate successfully, adopting measures to control them should mean one is able to control this main source of error in the clinical data. The Insufficiency Thesis (2) has already stated the measures to be adopted in the control of the suggestive influence of the analyst; namely, to follow the proper techniques of analytic therapy. Analysts are trained not to use suggestive language. They may be made more aware of the importance of giving their interpretations in the form of a hypothesis only. The analysand may accept or reject the interpretation, the truth of which is to be decided with the help of later evidence. The entire process of analysis is based on the assumption that P would acquire enough ego strength through the process of analysis to accept what is true about him.

However, this methodological procedure can be applied only with limited success. Sometimes for the sake of therapeutic purposes, the analyst may have to use suggestive language. In all such cases, resulting evidence may be accepted only after proper scrutiny regarding its evidential value. Also, in spite of the analyst's efforts to remain neutral and not use suggestive language or gestures, the analysand might still produce responses that he or she thinks will please the analyst. This may happen because of the strong state of suggestibility of P. This requires taking care that P is not in this state of strong suggestibility. For this, I propose the following: a truth demand from P be made an integral part of the analytic session.

As has been pointed out above, the state of suggestibility of P is one of the necessary conditions for the suggestive contamination of the data. This state again is endemic to the analytic situation. The state of suggestibility, by definition, consists in following the suggestions of the therapist, consciously or unconsciously. It depends on the therapist how he or she utilises the patient's state of suggestibility. I claim that if the charge of suggestibility is true then the state of suggestibility of P could be a means of the purification of the data rather than a source of its contamination. Almost no attention has been paid to this aspect of the state of suggestibility. But logically speaking this may be considered one of the best methods for controlling contamination of data directed towards the spurious confirmation of hypotheses. It should be realised that if P cannot be made to follow the instructions of the therapist, the entire charge of suggestibility is based on false logical grounds. Though conclusive evidence is not available, there is some evidence suggesting that an honesty demand helps in reducing the amount of exaggeration in the reports of task-motivated subjects. I cite here some of the experimental results of a demand for honesty on the verbal report of the subjects.

Bowers (1967) invented the demand for honesty from the subjects to test the validity of the verbal reports of subjects. He reappraised the results of an experiment done by Barber and Calverley (1964) in which the vividness of the hallucinatory experiences reported by a group of task-motivated subjects and a group of hypnotised subjects were considered. Apparently, the subjective ratings between the two groups did not differ significantly. However, it was to be ascertained whether the subjects were rating their genuine experiences or were merely complying with the instructions of the experimenter. In order to find an answer to this question, Bowers (1967) administered a demand for honesty in reporting subjective experiences. He instructed each subject that what was really wanted from them was what they really experienced. If they did not really hear or see things, they should not report it merely to please the experimenter.

> ... the results indicated that task-motivated subjects, when given these instructions, reported significantly less vivid hallucinatory experiences. (Wagstaff, 1981, p. 46)

Though there are differences in interpreting the results, another experiment performed by Spanos and Barber (1968) obtained the result that when honesty demands were not made, the task-motivational instructions increased the reports of vivid visual and auditory hallucination well above the baseline that was obtained before the start of the experiment. When honesty demands were made, such reports did not increase the vividness above the baseline.

When the hypnosis group were not asked to give honest reports, they also increased their reports above the baseline; however, when they were asked for honest reports they still increased their theory reports above baseline. The overall result has been interpreted by Bowers (1976) to mean that in the absence of honesty demands, the hypnotised subjects' reports of visual hallucinations were genuine whereas those of the task-motivated subjects were not (Wagstaff, 1981, p. 6).

Such reports suggest that it is possible to utilise the state of suggestibility of P for enforcing the accuracy of the data. This method can be used in controlling errors resulting from P's attempt to please the analyst and thus contaminate the data. For example, from the very beginning of the therapy, the analyst can emphasise that P should not try to please her but should give full, complete expression to whatever he is experiencing. In fact, this is what goes on in a genuine analytic session. Every psychoanalyst is familiar with the situation when a patient reveals some incident related to his or her life that had initially been "hidden" from the analyst. The patient reveals it at some point during analysis because of the honesty demand made by the analyst at the beginning of the treatment. But that is beside the point here. Such instructions may be repeated from time to time under appropriate circumstances. Analysts have to be careful so that P does not feel that his honesty is in question. This may adversely affect the treatment. But there are numerous occasions during the process of treatment when the point about truth and honesty can be made without additionally hurting the feelings of P.

How do we know whether a truth demand is effective in ensuring the objectivity of the data? Samples of sessions where a truth demand has been made and those where no such demand has been made can be compared to judge the efficacy of the method. A significant difference with respect to the variable of experiment would show whether the measures adopted are effective. A significant difference would imply that the data are not affected by the suggestive influence of the therapist to any significant degree. However, a truth demand alone might not be able to ensure the objectivity of the data to a reasonable extent. It does not take into account the subtle force of suggestion that might influence P and yet make him believe that what he is reporting is true.

To counter the effects of this factor, we adopt another principle that when a particular piece of evidence is suspected as having been influenced by the subtle suggestions of the analyst, independent evidence for the objectivity of the data should be obtained. Often such evidence can be obtained by comparing the different reports of the same state by P. If this is not possible, the evidence should be considered suspect. However, since the IT.2 basically suggests that the analysts do not use suggestive language, this, in combination with a truth demand, should reduce the degree of contamination of data in the clinical setting.

We can now restate the Insufficiency Thesis (2) in the following way: (IT.2′), which refers only to the situation occurring in the clinical setting:

> If the analyst in the analytic situation avoids suggestion and makes appropriate truth demands from P, it is highly unlikely that P will be experiencing a psychological state C at a time t (with all the associated and relevant psychological processes) consistently for a prolonged period of the therapy but he has never experienced C in reality or in phantasy at t′ where t′ is earlier than t.

We then have the following argument to counter the first part of the suggestibility charge; namely, the important sources of error in the data must be controlled. The argument states that to do this:

(i) The errors in memory reports can be checked with the help of the measures stated earlier, such as checking for consistency, etc. and then the frequency of errors can be estimated.
(ii) IT.2 can be used to control the more important problems of content implantation and biased evidence sifting.

To assess the objectivity and reliability of the data, any given analytic session can be recorded and assessed by judges. A high degree of inter-judge reliability should be considered sufficient proof for the acceptability of the data. Robert Holt, in *BBS Symposium* (1986) proposed that a more reliable method of judging the overall reliability of the data would be to record samples of clinical sessions and send them to pre-appointed judges who are expert psychoanalysts. These judges would be required to predict, on the bases of sample material, what kind of material they expect to emerge in the forthcoming sessions. These judges do not personally know either the patient or the analyst treating the patient. A high degree of successful prediction is good proof for the reliability of the data. Such a procedure was adopted by Bellak (1977). He reports:

> We were able to agree with satisfactory statistical validity and reliability on what forces were at play and predict what intervening forces would produce what effect in the future productions of a patient.

Silverman reports about the investigations of Sampson and Weiss and their co-workers:

> Their careful and well-controlled studies from tape recordings of treatment sessions have allowed them to isolate a crucial variable concerning analyst's behaviour that determines whether psychoanalytic sessions will proceed productively. (Silverman, 1985, p. 248)

Video recordings of the sessions would have been more reliable, since the gestures, facial expressions, movements, etc. contribute to a large degree to our assessment of the truth and falsity of a verbal report. However, this increases the chances of revealing the identity of P and hence is not often resorted to. One may still wonder whether this strengthening of IT.2 can save the situation. It is possible that avoidance of suggestion and truth-demand may help in a general way in lessening the degree of contamination. It is, however, doubtful whether this will make the data reliable enough for the purposes of theory validation.

The analyst has subtle influences over the analysand during the course of the therapy. The analysand is dependent on the analyst. The analyst's prestige and the high fee the analysand has to pay, as well as the analytic situation itself are all conducive for the subtle effects of suggestibility. Also, it is difficult to measure the effects of these influences. It is not possible, therefore, to know what proportion of the data is contaminated. However, the above objection overlooks one important point. The suggestive effect of the prestige of the analyst will be effective only temporarily. A treatment process in which P comes in contact with the analyst more than three days a week for years is likely to erode the overvaluation P might have attributed to the analyst. As time passes, P is more able to perceive the analyst in an objective way. The point can be tested by examining the samples of association from any analytic session.

Furthermore, such contamination of data occurs in the experimental situations also. Sources of some errors in experimental situations are similar to those in the clinical settings. The mere presence of the experimenter might introduce an uncontrolled variable. The experimenter with his subtle cues and movements might affect the performances of the subjects. There is some evidence that this is true. The very fact that the subjects are participating in experimental studies might affect their performance and bias the results in a given direction. Measures adopted to control these sources of error may themselves introduce new sources of errors. For example, to minimise the errors due to the bias of the experimenter, a single or double-blind study is performed. The subjects and the experimenters are both given false instructions about the objective of the study. This may prevent the experimenter from giving a subtle and unconscious cue to the subject regarding the desirability of his responses, but it may introduce a new source of bias. Even the celebrated study by Nisbett and Wilson on the inaccessibility of cognitive processes through introspection has been seriously criticised on methodological grounds.

> Nisbett and Wilson, in making this claim, are implicitly using an impossible criterion for introspective awareness: that subjects be aware of what we systematically and effectively hide from them by our experimental designs ... To take the fact that his methodology succeeds in hoaxing subjects and then to generate a general perceptual rule from it carries the point too far. (Smith & Miller, 1978, p. 356)

However, it might be objected that the bias in experimental studies is more controlled than in clinical settings. In spite of all the precautions mentioned above, the data obtained in the clinical setting are still not sufficiently reliable.

At this stage, the question is no longer the justifiability of using the clinical data for the purposes of theory validation. It becomes part of a broader question: how can we theoretically justify any testing procedure where there are known uncontrolled sources of error? To provide this justification, I shall refer to the theory of error proposed by Henry Kyburg, Jr. Kyburg was a conventionalist and did not believe in the traditional method of testing and confirming a theory. However, his theory of error in a way captures the insight of hypothetico-deductive method and probably provides a justification for the contemporary scientific practices too.

Kyburg's theory of error

I have mentioned earlier that there are important sources of error even in carefully controlled studies, yet we continue to conduct such studies and accept their results, provided the studies do not violate the standard rules of scientific investigation. But these rules provide us with no justification for accepting the results of a study where we have controlled the major sources of error but we know that there are uncontrolled and unmeasurable sources of error present. Also, how do we know beforehand that our data are now reliable enough for a scientific investigation? We need some theoretical principle to justify our scientific practice. It is this principle that has been provided by Kyburg's theory of error. According to Kyburg, we accept a theory in our rational corpus of belief on the basis of its ability to contribute to our predictive observational content. In this respect, Kyburg's account does not differ much from the traditional concept of theory validation by the hypothetico-deductive method. This traditional concept of theory validation does adopt the criterion of correct prediction as one of the important bases of confirmation.

However, Kyburg proceeds as follows: given that all our observations are infected with error, no theory will be able to make predictions with absolute certainty. All our predictions will come true with a certain degree of probability. If the predictions of a certain theory T are true only with a very low degree of probability, the theory is not worth having in our rational corpus of belief. Thus, T will be accepted in our rational corpus of belief only if the probability of its true predictions is within our acceptable range.

How do we decide the acceptable range of probability for the true predictions of a given theory T? This "range of acceptability" is partly determined by the constraints of the theory itself. It is, according to Kyburg, highly context dependent. In physics, for example, the acceptable range for correct predictions would be quite high; predictions coming out true with the probability of [.9, 1.0]. In psychology, the acceptable range would be much lower, the reason being that there are greater instances of error in our observation reports in psychology. Thus, the subject matter of the theory puts constraints on the probability of correct predictions. However, it is the scientific community that decides the acceptable range of the probability of correct predictions of a given theory T and this decision is partly determined by the context.

According to Kyburg, this process of finding out the probability of correct predictions of a theory T proceeds with the following principles: (a) the minimisation principle, and (b) the distribution principle. The minimisation principle requires that we attribute no more errors to our observation than our theory requires us to. Thus, if T is: all ravens are black, we can have only two types of error. Some of our erroneous observations would be related to errors regarding the kind of bird we have observed; others regarding the colour of the bird.

The distribution principle requires that we distribute these errors as smoothly as possible. In other words, we distribute them in the form of a normal probability curve. On the bases of these principles, we shall be able to obtain data regarding the frequency of errors of various sorts. Statistical inference based on these data will give us the long term error rates. This will help us in controlling the sources of error. For example, we find that if we observe ravens when dusk is approaching we tend to make more errors related to the colour of the bird and so on. We can control these sources of error once we can isolate them.

Error rates are determined by theories. A theory whose predictions are unreliable is eschewed and not accepted in our rational corpus. If we apply this proposal to our current scientific practices we can provide justification for conducting studies even though there may be unknown sources of error. For example, in the case of the theory "smoking causes lung cancer", the minimisation principle requires that only two types of errors—namely, those related to smoking and those related to cancer—be taken into account. After we have distributed these errors and found out the long-run error rates of various sorts, we can control various sources of error. For example, we can find out that unreliable predictions result if we take into account only the numbers of cigarettes smoked and do not take into account whether the smoke was inhaled. In this way, we can find out the errors of various sorts and control them. The acceptance of the theory in our rational corpus of belief will finally depend on the reliability of its predictions. In our scientific investigation of smoking and cancer, this is exactly what we are doing. We take care of the known sources of error related to our theory. This gives us a more reliable measure of the long-run frequency of error. With the help of this we can compute the predictability with which the predictions of the theory should come out true. If after controlling those sources the predictions of the theory fall below the range of acceptability, we would not accept the theory in its present form.

The advantage of having this minimisation principle is that we will no longer have to determine beforehand whether our observations are free from all sources of error. We will know of those sources of error that are related to our theory, and we will have taken care of those. This gives us a method of computing the probability with which our predictions should come out true. For example, the theory predicts that people smoking X number of cigarettes per day have Y probability of suffering from lung cancer. If the actual occurrence of cancer among smokers does not bear out this prediction of T, T may be considered unreliable and eschewed in its present form.

Thus, by accepting the minimisation principle, we can justify our temporary acceptance of the results of studies done on cancer and smoking even though we know that there is a confounding variable of heredity. If our long-run observations show that the predictions of the theory are unreliable, we give up the theory. In a way, all our acceptance of clinical results is temporary. We accept conclusions that are based on strong evidence but have not been conclusively proven. New evidence may refute the previous conclusion.

A similar approach can be taken in the case of a psychoanalytic clinical setting. Suppose, our T is: paranoid delusions are causally related to repressed homosexuality. The minimisation principle requires that we take care of two important kinds of error: those related to paranoid delusions, and those related to the observation of repressed homosexuality. Our background knowledge dictates that the suggestion of the analyst is an important source of error in our observation of repressed homosexuality in P. We control these sources of error by taking the precautions I have mentioned above. There still remains the factor of the subtle suggestion of the analyst, an uncontrolled source of error like the confounding variable of heredity in cancer-smoking studies. However, after controlling these sources of error, we can find out whether the predictions of the theory turn out to be true with a fair degree of reliability. If not, the theory in its present form may be abandoned. We may have reason to suppose that, probably, the subtle influence of the analyst was somehow connected with the evidence of repressed homosexuality.

We are, however, faced with a problem here. The prediction of the cancer-smoking theory can be observed openly and publicly. If the theory predicts that a person who smokes so many packs of cigarettes in a day has a given degree of probability of suffering from cancer, the correctness of this prediction can be observed in any observational situation. But if a psychoanalyst makes a similar prediction, the correctness of the prediction cannot be observed in an extra-clinical setting. Repressed homosexuality is not a phenomenon that can be observed by anyone publicly. It requires that the repression be removed and the homosexual desires be made conscious. This is a task that is performed in the psychoanalytic clinical setting. The clinical setting is fraught with the subtle suggestions of the analyst. If the correctness of the predictions be judged on the basis of clinical data, the rate of successful predictions will always be very high and we would accept the theory in our rational corpus. But should we? Isn't it possible that the successful predictions are due to the subtle suggestive influence of the analyst? It may be objected that unless observations are made in such a way that the subtle influence of the analyst be removed, we can never be certain that the rate of successful predictions is due to the truth of the theory.

But the objection is totally inapplicable here. When we are making observations regarding the rate of cancer and smoking, it is true that we are not making observations in a testing situation. But our observations are made under circumstances where the confounding variable of heredity is always present. But presence of a confounding variable does not totally invalidate the results of our study. We do accept those results in a probabilistic way, keeping in mind that further studies need to be conducted to test the reliability of the results.

We are liable to get contrary evidence if we try to duplicate our studies in widely varied circumstances. If there is an inherent bias in our observation, chances are that large sampling will bring it out. Until that happens, the minimisation principle justifies our conducting scientific studies and accepting their results probabilistically. The demand that all the known sources of error must be controlled and the data must be known to be reliable beyond all doubt is too strict a demand and will put an end to all our scientific endeavours.

I conclude, therefore, that the suggestibility charge as stated by Grünbaum ignores the fact that in no scientific studies are data ever completely free from error. Psychoanalytic clinical data are not unique in this sense. In answering the suggestibility charge we have to be careful not to make suggestions on par with "Descartes' evil demon". Suggestion is not all-powerful. If it were, the world would have been a happier place to live in. In my next chapter, I shall answer Grünbaum's objection related to the validity of the psychoanalytic arguments.

Note

1. I am indebted to Prof. Otto Thaler of the University of Rochester, Rochester, NY, for the clarification of this point.

PART II

CHAPTER FIVE

Is Freud guilty of faulty reasoning?*

Section I

As I have mentioned previously, Grünbaum's attack on psychoanalysis is concentrated on two fronts. If I am permitted to use the language of deductive logic, Grünbaum is trying to show that the arguments supporting the major psychoanalytic hypotheses are both unsound and invalid. The suggestibility charge was intended to show that the psychoanalytic arguments are unsound. Translated in the language of inductive logic, this amounts to showing that the conclusions of these arguments are not well-supported by the evidence. In previous chapters, I have argued that the suggestibility charge against psychoanalysis is highly exaggerated. I have shown that the Tally Argument, the main pillar of attack by Grünbaum, does not correctly represent the position of Freud or the theoretical implications of psychoanalysis. I have also argued how by adopting proper techniques and statistical measures the suggestibility charge can be handled to a great extent.

---

*This chapter was based on a paper I read titled "The Repression Argument and Grünbaum" at the Centre for the Philosophy of Science, University of Pittsburgh, Pittsburgh, Pennsylvania, in 1994.

We now come to the second part of Grünbaum's attack on psychoanalysis. In this part, Grünbaum has tried to establish that even if the validity of the data were not in question, the reasoning on which Freud rested his major clinical hypotheses—its edifice—is fundamentally flawed (see Grünbaum, 1986).

Grünbaum has selected three major hypotheses of psychoanalysis to prove the above claim. These are:

- The hypothesis that repressed conflict is the cause of psychoneuroses.
- The hypothesis that repressed conflict is the cause of parapraxes.
- The hypothesis that repressed childhood desires are the cause of dreams.

The common link is the theory of repression. In my response to Grünbaum, I shall deal only with the first hypothesis.

While a number of attempts have been made to refute his Tally Argument related to the contamination of clinical data, his objection against the repression aetiology remains largely unanswered. In this chapter, I shall discuss his objections against the repression aetiology of psychoneuroses and show that they are untenable. It is to be noted that in his book *Validation in the Clinical Theory of Psychoanalysis* (1993) (henceforth referred to as *Validation*) Grünbaum has not substantially changed his views regarding the Tally Argument or regarding his "Repression Argument". Grünbaum has reconstructed Freud's argument for repression aetiology. This reconstruction is based upon the account given in *Studies on Hysteria* (1895d), a joint publication of Freud and Breuer.

The repression argument

The causal hypothesis arrived at by Freud in collaboration with Breuer is related to the aetiology of hysteria. Breuer's patient Anna O. was relieved of her neurotic symptoms after she recalled, under hypnosis, forgotten episodes that were thematically related to her symptoms. On the basis of this evidence, Freud and Breuer concluded that the lifting of repression was the cause of the cure. Grünbaum reconstructed Freud and Breuer's repression argument in the following way:

(1) Lifting of a repression R of an event E is followed by the cure of neurotic symptom S;

(2) therefore, lifting of a repression R of E is sufficient condition for the cure of S.
(3) If lifting of R of E is causally sufficient for the cure of S, then an original repression of E is causally necessary for the formation of S; and
(4) an ongoing coexisting repression of E is causally necessary for the maintenance of the symptom S.

As he says in *Foundations*:

> Thus, the nub of their inductive argument for inferring repression etiology can be formulated as follows: the *removal* of a hysterical symptom S *by means of lifting* a repression R is *cogent evidence* that the repression R was *causally necessary* for the formation of the symptom S (S. E., 1893, 2:7). For if an ongoing repression R was causally necessary for the pathogenesis *and* persistence of a neurosis N, then the removal of R must issue in the eradication of N. Hence the inferred etiology yielded a deductive explanation of the supposed remedial efficacy of undoing repressions. (p. 179)

Grünbaum emphasises that it was necessary for Freud and Breuer to postulate repression for both the origin and maintenance of the symptom S, otherwise they could not explain why the lifting of repression R of E would lead to the removal of S. He points out:

> In any case, at the time, Breuer and Freud believed that their therapeutic results had ruled out the dangerous rival hypothesis of placebo effect by suggestion. And this belief did figure, as we saw, in their reasoning, when they concluded the following: (1) an *ongoing* coexisting repression is causally necessary for the *maintenance* of a neurosis N, and (2) an *original* act of repression was the causal *sine qua non* for the *origination* of N. (*Foundations*, p. 180)

According to Grünbaum, this reasoning is fraught with the following logical difficulties: In passing from (1) to (2) of the repression argument Freud and Breuer have committed the fallacy of post hoc ergo propter hoc. Their conclusion that the cure was due to the lifting of repression is unwarranted according to the inductive criterion of justification of causal inferences. Freud and Breuer have failed to rule out the rival hypothesis that the cure could be due to the suggestion of the therapist. The patient was aware that Breuer attached special significance to the recall of the event with which the symptoms started. This awareness on the part of the patient might have led her to produce thematically related memories with each symptom and be cured. Thus, the cure could still be due to the subtle suggestion conveyed by the physician rather than due to the lifting of repression.

In order to avoid the fallacy of post hoc ergo proper hoc, Grünbaum says, it is essential to compare the results of the treatment gains of a group whose repression has been lifted (the experimental group) with the results of the treatment gains of a comparable control group whose repression has not been lifted. Since Freud and Breuer did not compare their results with a control group, the possibility that the cure could be due to the placebo of suggestion cannot be ruled out.

Even if we grant for the sake of argument, continues Grünbaum, that the lifting of R of E was causally sufficient for the cure, it still does not follow that R of E was causally necessary for the original formation of the symptom. In other words, the step from (2) to (3) is invalid. As Morris Eagle has pointed out, says Grünbaum, R might have been causally necessary for the *maintenance* of the symptom only and not for the *origin* of the symptom. Thus, if we grant the validity of the premise that lifting of repression R of E is sufficient condition for the cure of S, then the claim that an ongoing repression necessary for the maintenance of the symptom follows, but the claim of an original repression of event E necessary for the origin of the symptom does not follow. It may still be true that the conscious experience of the event E caused the symptom and an anxiety produced by it caused the repression. Hence, it is E that is causally necessary for S, not R of E. The repression R of E is merely the maintaining cause of S, devoid of all aetiological role. The causal inference, therefore, is not justified.

This distinction between a maintaining cause and an originating cause is very important for Grünbaum's argument against Freud. Grünbaum says that Freud has used the hypothetico-deductive method as his criterion of scientific validation. Grünbaum says in *Validation*:

> Avowedly, his (Freud's) ideals *or* criteria of scientific validation are roughly those of hypothetico-deductive or quasi-statistical inductivism and he took adherence to them to be the hallmark of the scientific probity he claimed for his theory … I shall grant Freud

> his own canon of scientific status in addressing the following key question: Did his clinical arguments vindicate the knowledge claims he made for his evolving theory by labelling it "scientific"?
>
> My answer will be twofold: The reasoning on which Freud rested the major hypotheses of his edifice was fundamentally flawed, even if the probity of the clinical observations he adduced were not in question. (p. 20)

Grünbaum proceeds to say that Freud's argument can be proved faulty by his own canon. Hypothetico-deductive method often leads to conclusions that are causally irrelevant. For example, on the basis of a perfectly legitimate hypothesis that taking oral contraceptive pills prevents pregnancy, we may conclude that Mr X has not become pregnant because he was mistakenly taking the oral contraceptive pills of his wife.

It is this charge of irrelevancy that Grünbaum considers relevant against the repression argument. According to him, from arguing that the lifting of repression is a sufficient condition for cure to arguing that an original act of repression is a necessary condition for the formation and maintenance of symptom S, Freud and Breuer may have overlooked the fact that repression may be totally irrelevant for the aetiology of neuroses. It may merely be that the maintaining cause is devoid of all aetiological significance while the conscious experience of the traumatic event could be the cause of the "initial formation" of the symptom. Morris Eagle's argument, therefore, is very important for Grünbaum to show the causal irrelevancy of repression in neuroses.

Grünbaum further says that the illegitimacy of this argument was soon borne out by subsequent events. It turned out that when Freud applied cathartic method later in his therapy, the therapeutic results were not encouraging. Recall of a traumatic event related with the origin of the symptom did not result in a lasting cure. Freud thus abandoned the claim that the lifting of the repression of a traumatic event E is causally sufficient for the lasting removal of S. But he did not abandon his repression aetiology. Instead, he continued to search for earlier repressed memories, which may be causally connected with the symptom. In other words, Freud continued to maintain that the repression of some event or other is causally necessary for a neurotic symptom S. The recall of the event with which symptoms started was termed merely the occasioning trauma or the precipitating cause.

Not only this, Grünbaum argues, there was decisive counter-evidence for repression aetiology that Freud totally ignored, continuing to maintain his hypothesis in the face of adverse evidence. The adverse evidence was provided by Freud's admission that the cure of the symptoms was associated with the patients' positive attitude towards the therapist. Freud reports in his 1925 *Autobiographical Study*:

> ... even the most brilliant results were liable to be suddenly wiped away if my personal relation with the patient became disturbed. It was true that they would be re-established if a reconciliation could be effected; but such an occurrence proved that the personal emotional relation between doctor and patient was after all stronger than the whole cathartic process ... (Freud, 1925d, p. 27)

According to Grünbaum, this was decisive counter-evidence for the repression aetiology. Freud's own admission establishes the following two points:

(i) Therapeutic gain was not invariably associated with the lifting of repression R of E;
(ii) therapeutic gain was invariably associated both positively and negatively with good relations with the therapist.

According to Grünbaum, the first point falsified the very premise, the sole evidence of cure, on which repression aetiology was based. With the evidence gone, there is no empirical support for the hypothesis. The second point provides decisive counter-evidence for repression aetiology. If the therapeutic gains are not causally related with the lifting of the repression but depend decisively on the relationship of the patient with the doctor, then there is no justification for continuing to believe that some repression or other is causally necessary for the formation of the symptom. As Grünbaum says:

> In short, I claim that *the moral of Freud's therapeutic disappointment in the use of cathartic method after 1893 was nothing less than the collapse of the epoch-making argument for the repression aetiology of neurosis*, which Breuer and he had propounded. (*Foundations*, pp. 183–184, italics in original)

This is, in brief, Grünbaum's argument that Freud's reasoning for the repression aetiology is faulty and that his argument supporting the repression aetiology is logically flawed. Theory of repression is the cornerstone of psychoanalysis. By arguing that the logical status of the theory of repression is flawed, Grünbaum is, in fact, arguing that the whole theory is based on faulty logical grounds. I shall now argue that Grünbaum's objections are untenable; that it is possible to formulate a valid argument for repression aetiology.

Section II

Are Grünbaum's objections valid?

It is to be noted that the repression argument is merely partly historical. It is based upon Freud's reasoning but is treated as the representative of the current logical status of psychoanalysis. Grünbaum says:

> The appraisal (of psychoanalytic theory) concentrates on the central arguments offered by the founding father, because his own reasoning, though deeply flawed, is considerably more challenging than most of the defenses by his later exponents. (*BBS Symposium*, p. 217)

In other words, in claiming that the repression argument is logically faulty, Grünbaum is claiming that this logical fault is carried over to the present status of psychoanalysis also and that psychoanalysis is unable to provide any acceptable argument for the justification of repression aetiology.

Grünbaum is right in saying that Breuer and Freud were too quick in dismissing the suggestion hypothesis. Later when Freud had given up the cathartic method and developed what is today known as psychoanalysis, he admitted that the cure of Anna O. was probably brought about by intense transference that she had developed towards Breuer (1914). But at the time *Studies on Hysteria* was written the phenomenon of transference was as yet unknown. Thus, Grünbaum's objection in this respect is justified.

Before answering Grünbaum's charge against repression aetiology, I would like to make the following point: in recent years a lot has been made of the fact that Anna O. was admitted to a sanatorium—three times during a period of five years after Breuer discontinued her treatment—without taking into account why and with what symptoms she was admitted. Grünbaum says:

> Yet after all is said and done, the Anna O. case does not deserve the place it received above in the debate on placebogenic gain: As we know from Ellenberger (1972) and Hirschmüller (1989), Breuer's treatment of hers turned out to be a fiasco. (*Validation*, p. 240)

It is a little surprising that Grünbaum should mention Hirschmüller in this context. In this very well researched book on the life and work of Josef Breuer, Hirschmüller has given the complete text of a letter written by Breuer to Dr Binswanger—the director of the sanatorium where Anna O. was admitted after Breuer discontinued her treatment. This letter lists the symptoms that were cured by him. It appears that all the symptoms with which Anna O. was suffering when Breuer took over her treatment and that Breuer has mentioned in *Studies on Hysteria* were cured and never returned. Anna O. also suffered from trigeminal neuralgia, which is not a psychological disorder. She was given a high dosage of morphine by Breuer and had become addicted to it.

Dr Laupus, Assistant Physician at Bellevue Clinic, describes the following symptoms of Anna O.: trigeminal neuralgia; genuine signs of hysteria manifested in unintentional fluctuation of mood; her exaggerated mourning for her father; expressing her phantasies in the form of fairy tales; and during the evening, loss of her mother tongue. Anna O. herself in a letter written in English from the sanatorium describes her symptoms in the following way: (i) inability to speak, read or understand her native language German; (ii) strong neuralgic pain; (iii) shorter or longer absences accompanied by a strong feeling of "time-missing". Hirschmüller very clearly says that aphasia was the only symptom that, contrary to Breuer's claim, was not completely cured. However, if aphasia is the inability to use language, then a person who could speak three languages (in the evening Anna O. spoke fluent English, French, and Italian) could hardly be characterised as suffering from aphasia.

Hirschmüller's book certainly does not give the impression that Anna O.'s treatment was a "fiasco" as claimed by Grünbaum. As a person and as a physician Breuer's honesty was above reproach. Hirschmüller thinks that most probably Breuer thought that the symptoms, which were of psychological origin, had all been taken care of. The findings certainly give the impression that severe neuralgic pain and addiction to morphine was the most prominent symptoms for which she needed institutionalisation. She was discharged from the sanatorium the first time because no improvement could be brought about either regarding her neuralgic pain or her morphine addiction. It is not clear how she finally overcame it. It was in January 1884 that Breuer comments to Dr Binswanger, "I saw the young Pappenheim girl today. She is in good health, no pains or other trouble". The comment leads one to believe that neuralgic pain was the most important, if not the only reason, to institutionalise Anna O. Trigeminal neuralgia and addiction to morphine are not psychological in origin. Anna O. did have some hysterical symptoms also—minor compared to what she was suffering from when Breuer took over her treatment (see Hirschmüller, 1989, p. 295).[1]

I come back to Grünbaum's argument. Grünbaum objects that Freud maintained his repression aetiology even in the face of adverse evidence. The correlation between two properties A and B both positively and negatively is generally a good indication of a causal relation between them but is not always decisive evidence of such a relation. This has long been modified to assert that if C and E have been found to be associated both in presence and in absence, then it is justified to infer that C and E are causally related provided there is no variable G that screens off the association between C and E.

In this particular case there was ample reason to believe that the following two hypotheses may be true: first, the doctor-patient relationship itself could be the product of earlier childhood repression. This was a reasonable hypothesis also. Freud was surprised at the nature and intensity of feelings with which this relationship emerged during the course of treatment, though there was nothing in the behaviour of the doctor to warrant the development of such intense feelings on the part of the patient.

Second, the doctor-patient relationship was interfering with the proper unearthing of relevant repression. It is to be noted that the treatment gains that were attributed to the doctor-patient relationship did not lead to permanent cure. The gains were temporary and fragile; very similar in nature to those obtained through hypnotic therapy. Therefore, it was possible that hypnotism, which was the method of therapy, may be responsible for obscuring the course of treatment.

These hypotheses were worth investigating, and giving up repression aetiology before such investigations were carried out would have been premature. Therefore, the apparent correlation between therapeutic gain and good relations between doctor and patient does not provide conclusive evidence for giving up repression aetiology. In fact, it would be too naive for any scientist merely to rely on the evidence of a double agreement. This agreement provides us with good grounds to believe that there is a causal relation between the observed properties, but the rule should be accepted with caution. Given the possibility of a common cause, or a screener-off, Freud was perfectly justified in considering the doctor-patient relationship not being the decisive causal factor in the cure of P and not giving up repression aetiology.

Grünbaum has offered two major objections against the repression argument, which I restate here. The repression argument violates the principles of eliminative induction. It fails to eliminate the two rival causal hypotheses: (i) the hypothesis that repression could be the maintaining and not the originating cause of the symptom S; and (ii) the placebo hypothesis that cure could be due to suggestion.

The first objection is based upon a distinction between the "originating cause" of a symptom S and the "maintaining cause" of S. To assert that any given effect is produced by one causal entity and maintained by another causal entity is to claim that there are two distinct causal entities operating at a given point in time for the effect to manifest. According to the principle of parsimony, entities should be postulated for the explanation of a given phenomenon only if they are either *empirically* or *rationally* justified. The assertion of two causal entities, thus, needs some justification, empirical or rational. If no such justification is found, we shall reject the claim.

Also, in order to make this distinction comprehensible, the following points should be kept in mind: it is important to clarify the sense in which "originating cause" and "maintaining cause" are used. Because there is a sense in which Freud certainly would not object to admitting that the event E was the originating cause of S. Freud would admit that the anxiety produced by the conscious experience of E led to the repression of E and the repression of E led to S. Hence, if there was no E, there would have been no repression of E and consequently no S. From this point of view, E is certainly the originating cause of the whole chain. But this is not the sense in which "originating cause" and "maintaining cause" have been used by Grünbaum, as we shall see later.

This distinction between originating and maintaining cause raised another question: at what point in time does the origin of an effect E cease and the maintenance of E begin? Does it start simultaneously? The latter seems more reasonable. The effect E is being maintained even while it is originated. If E is not maintained from the point of its origin there would be nothing left to maintain. Therefore, if the originating and maintaining causes are different entities, both must be present from the beginning of the effect E. We shall also assume that such a distinction is applicable only in some cases and not in all cases. The stronger assumption will be easy to falsify. So, we are ascribing a weaker assumption to Grünbaum that is difficult to falsify. However, Grünbaum needs to provide us with some justification for this multiplication of ontological entities in those cases where such a distinction is introduced. What then are the rational or empirical justifications for the introduction of this distinction between an originating and a maintaining cause in the case of a neurotic symptom S? A rational justification in this case would be to show that we would fail to derive the correct logical conclusion without assuming the existence of the postulated causal entity.

But this certainly is not the case here. If the destruction of the tubercular bacillus T is a sufficient condition for the cure of TB, we infer that being infected with T is a necessary condition for contracting TB. So, by manipulating the presence or absence of T, we manipulate the presence or absence of tuberculosis. Hence, we are justified in ascribing a causal role to the tubercular bacilli. Similarly, if by manipulating the presence or absence of repression we can manipulate the "maintenance or non-maintenance of S", where non-maintenance of S is identical to the non-existence of S, we can ascribe a causal role to the lifting of repression with respect to S.

When Grünbaum asserts that the event E may be the cause of the initial formation of S and repression of E could merely be its maintaining cause having no aetiological significance, his assertion implies that experience of an event E is a necessary condition for the initial formation of S, but repression of E is a necessary condition only for the maintenance of S. This poses a significant problem. Since the existence of an event and its repression do not always occur simultaneously, there would be a possible state of affairs where a symptom S is originated but not maintained. It is to be noted that repression R of the event E is not a necessary condition for the initial formation of S. Hence, S could originate without R of E—that is, without the repression of the event E.

In all such cases, we have instances of S at the moment of its initial formation, but S is not maintained because E is not repressed.

It is difficult to understand how things would go under such circumstances. What does it mean to say that S is originated but not maintained? If S is not maintained, does it exist? If it does not exist, can we talk about a symptom S for which a therapeutic procedure might be needed?

It seems to me that when we are talking about symptoms, we are talking about behaviours that persist over some length of time—that is, the behaviour/or mental state in question has to be maintained. The length of duration for which it is maintained is not significant. It is difficult to provide a minimum time frame for which it must be maintained. Without maintenance of behaviour for some length of time there is no behaviour and there is no symptom. Why, then, is the factor responsible for the maintenance devoid of any causal role? Furthermore, one can hardly worry about the cure of a "symptom" that is not maintained. In fact, how can one recognise a behaviour to be a "symptom" if it is not maintained?

Thus, Grünbaum's assertion that E could be the cause of the initial formation of S while repression of E the maintaining cause is not justified. Without the maintenance of S, there is no behaviour and there is no symptom. Therefore, whatever factor is responsible for the maintenance of S is the factor that is of causal significance from an empirical point of view. A behavioural manifestation or a psychological state that is not maintained over any length of time does not require any special attention on our part, or any special preventive measures.

However, Grünbaum might object to the above discussion by pointing out (i) that his distinction is intended to apply only to cases where a symptom has already been formed and maintained, and not to those cases where a symptom has not been maintained; (ii) his case differs from the case of tubercular bacilli where the originating and the maintaining causes were the same; namely, the bacillus T. But in the case of neurotic symptoms there are two distinct entities: the conscious experience of a traumatic event E and its repression R. Therefore, his case differs significantly from that of tubercular bacilli.

His argument can be reformulated in the following way: in all cases where there is a neurotic symptom S, E is the cause of the initial formation of S and repression of E is the cause of the maintenance of S. This position also involves significant empirical problems. In order to understand the problems involved, we shall discuss a similar instance in epidemiology where two different causal factors have been hypothesised for a given effect. For example:

> Doll and Pike have each postulated that the neoplastic transformation of a number of individual cells is necessary in order to produce a "nest" of transformed cells which constitute the beginning of a tumour. ... It is also possible that a carcinogenic agent initiated a malignant transformation that requires an additional promoting agent for further growth of the malignancy. Thus, an individual is exposed at a specific point in time to an initiating agent that transforms the cell, and only after an interval of years does exposure to a promoting agent occur, which stimulates growth leading to a malignant tumour. (Lilienfeld & Lilienfeld, 1980, p. 57)

The hypothesis quoted above is a perfectly legitimate and reasonable one. It can be stated more precisely in the following way:

- Exposure to a carcinogenic agent X at a given time t is a necessary condition for the initial transformation of normal cells into carcinogenic cells C.
- Exposure of C to a growth-promoting agent Y at a later time t′ is a necessary condition for the growth of cancerous cells into a malignant tumour.

The above points imply the following:

- Non-exposure to X at any time t is a sufficient condition for the non-transformation of the normal cells into carcinogenic cells C.
- Non-exposure of C to Y at a later time t′ is a sufficient condition for the non-growth of the cancerous cells into a malignant tumour.

This would imply, however, that the removal of a growth-promoting agent would stop the growth of the tumour only, not the initial transformation of the cells early in life. If there is no neoplastic transformation of cells, the exposure to Y will not result in a tumour.

If the removal of Y results not only in the prevention of the growth of a tumour but also affects the initial transformation of the cells, it would be negative evidence for the hypothesis. The hypothesis that two separate causal factors are responsible for the initial transformation and later growth of the cells into cancer respectively is a combination of two hypotheses and both the hypotheses need testing in order to be empirically justified. The epidemiological methods for testing such hypotheses are well known and do not require illustration here. In fact, similar hypotheses have been tested in epidemiology. As Lilienfeld and Lilienfeld remark:

> That this sequence of events occurs in human biology is well recognized. X-radiation and a variety of chemical and viruses, for example, may produce a neo-plastic transformation of the cells resulting in clinical cancer. Many other agents may also produce cellular mutations resulting in clinical cancer. (Lilienfeld & Lilienfeld, 1980, p. 293)

Grünbaum's hypothesis based upon the distinction between originating and maintaining causes is similar to the above hypothesis except that instead of a growth-promoting agent he posits a maintaining-cause agent. In order to justify this hypothesis we have to justify that:

- A traumatic event E is a necessary condition for the initial formation of the symptom S.
- Repression of traumatic event E is a necessary condition for the maintenance of S.

We already have evidence for the second point, as Grünbaum agrees. Removal of the repression R of E results in the removal of the symptom S. So, removal of the repression of E is a sufficient condition for the non-maintenance of the symptom. Therefore, RE is a necessary condition for the maintenance of S.

How can we have evidence that E was the cause of the initial formation of the symptom S? All that one can say in this case is that when a symptom is present, it must have been formed. And if by removing repression we remove all traces of symptom, then there does not seem to be any justification for assuming that there was a separate, distinct causal factor responsible for the initial formation of S. The present case is also significantly different from the epidemiological case presented above. Even in the absence of a growth-promoting agent the clinical cancer exists and its existence can be tested by clinically approved methods. But in the absence of a so-called maintaining cause, there is no symptom.

However, there is another way in which one may try to find evidence that E was the cause for the initial formation of S. If P is not exposed to the traumatic event E and does not develop S, while significant numbers of those who have been exposed to E develop S, this would be strong evidence that E is causally related to S. But even this evidence is not obtainable, if P is not exposed to E there would be no repression of E. Hence, one would not know whether it was the absence of E or absence of RE that is causally responsible for the non-occurrence of S. On the other hand, the positive association between exposure to E and S does not warrant the conclusion that it was E that was causally responsible for S for obvious reasons. Thus, it is almost impossible to empirically justify one component of Grunbaum's claim that in all cases of neurotic symptom S, an initial traumatic event E is the originating and a repression R of the event E is the maintaining cause of S.

However, in spite of all this, Grünbaum's point may be a slightly different one that may be explained with the help of the following examples. Consider the following:

- Rich catches a cold and Andrea asks him to rest. Rich continues to work. The symptoms of a cold also continue. Andrea says that Rich's going to work is the maintaining cause of the cold though she is perfectly aware that some viral infection is the originating cause of the cold.
- Jee Loo breaks her leg. After her leg is taken out of the cast her doctor asks her to do some exercises to remove the rigidity of the leg muscles. Jee Loo does not do the exercises. The doctor says that Jee Loo's not doing the exercises is the maintaining cause of her pain though she is perfectly aware that the rigidity of the leg muscles is the originating cause of her pain.
- Ann is suffering from tuberculosis. She refuses to take antibiotics. The doctor says that not taking the medication is the maintaining cause of Ann's continued affliction.

It makes sense to talk about maintaining causes in the above and similar cases. What is intended to be conveyed in the above examples can be expressed in a counterfactual way; if Rich had taken rest and Jee Loo had done her exercises and Ann had taken her medications all three of them would have recovered. Maybe this is the sense in which Grünbaum is using the concept of maintaining cause. Maybe he wants to say that if P hadn't repressed, he would have recovered from his symptoms. Maybe it is reasonable to talk about such causes in general, and it is possible that such causes are operative in the case of neurotic symptoms as well. If so, repression could very well be the maintaining cause of P's symptoms and could be completely devoid of aetiological significance.

Let us try to see what is really happening in the above examples. It makes sense to say that going to work is the maintaining cause of cold symptoms. It also makes sense to say that not doing exercises recommended by the doctor is the maintaining cause of leg pain. But it makes equal sense to say that the presence of a virus in the body is the maintaining cause of the cold symptoms and the persistence of muscular rigidity is the maintaining cause of the pain in the leg. It also makes sense to say that the continued presence of tubercular bacilli in the body is the maintaining cause of Ann's tuberculosis. What we are asserting is that the recommended actions are considered "instrumental" in removing the maintaining causes, which are identical with the originating causes of the respective symptoms.

These "instrumental causes" are neither necessary nor sufficient conditions for the maintenance of S. Rich may continue to work, but his cold symptoms are highly likely to disappear if he takes the new medicine that has been invented by a British doctor and has been found to be effective in 99% of cases of cold symptoms. Realising Jee Loo's aversion to exercise, the doctor may recommend her the new high-tech but very expensive programme where electrodes attached to leg muscles massage and relax muscles within a day, resulting in the disappearance of the pain. Thus, all these methods are instrumental. The same is true in the case of Ann not taking the antibiotics. She may be put on a diet programme in which the chemical components of the antibiotic are ingested by her through the natural process of food intake, resulting in her eventual release from the symptoms of tuberculosis.

Thus, all these methods are instrumental only. They are instrumental in eliminating the necessary conditions for the symptoms. They are not necessary either for the origin or for the maintenance of the symptom itself. But, as Grünbaum claims, both the repression of an event E and conscious experience of E are necessary for the manifestation of a symptom. Thus, this argument also fails to provide a justification for the introduction of multiple causal entities in the case of neurotic symptoms.

Now, let us suppose that it is legitimate in some cases to grant the existence of this dual causality. We would then like to know how and in what way it would affect our causal investigation. In our causal investigations we are primarily interested in knowing whether by manipulating a given factor or property we are able to prevent or produce another property as the case may be. As Kyburg puts it:

> It is true that not all causes are such that we could manipulate them: we may know the cause of a disease without being able either to cure it or prevent it. But … to know the cause is to see the possibility of manipulating it. To know that you built the fire, is to be in a position to ask you to put it out; … to know that sympathetic vibrations are the cause of the failure of a bridge is not to know how to avoid them in the next bridge, but it is the first step; to know that a certain organism causes the disease that concerns us is to know that if we could destroy that organism then we could prevent or cure that disease. (Kyburg, [typed manuscript, p. 275, subsequently published by OUP, 1990])

In other words: Is this distinction between the originating and maintaining cause empirically significant? Does it provide us with extra knowledge in the manipulation of the so-called causal factors? I shall answer this question with reference to neurotic symptoms only. Grünbaum may argue that if one knows that the event E is the necessary condition for the initial formation of S one may try to prevent E so that symptoms are not formed in the first place; then we will not have to worry about the persistence of the symptoms at all. This may bring about a significant difference in our preventive measures.

It is not clear what kind of significant difference it will make. The best way to prevent the repression of E also is to prevent the occurrence of E. After all, repression is not repression of nothing but of the memory of the conscious experience of a concrete event accompanied by intense affects. So, if P is not subjected to such events, there would be no need for him to take recourse to repression. Thus, so far as preventive measures for neuroses are concerned both the approaches lead us to the same result.

However, the matter is not over yet. Grünbaum may argue that since the event E is necessary for the production of a symptom but not for its maintenance over any length of time, S will disappear as soon as it appears if there is no repression. But after S has appeared once because of a certain event E, in future we may take preventive measures so that the individual is not subjected to such events. One may also generalise on the basis of such experience; for example, event E has been found to produce S in P, hence E is neurosogenic and individuals should not be put in such situations.

This argument fails to save the situation. Let us take two possible cases:

(1) P undergoes a traumatic experience E that gives rise to S. E is repressed. If E is repressed, S is maintained. The purpose of prevention is not served.
(2) P undergoes a traumatic experience E that gives rise to S. E is not repressed. Hence, S is not maintained. In future, we may prevent the occurrence of E to prevent the occurrence of S.

But the second case is plausible only if S is maintained. If it is not maintained, is there an S? And if so, do we care for expensive preventive measures? It follows that without the presence of R of E there is no maintenance of S, and without maintenance of S there is no S to deal with. Therefore, this distinction between originating and maintaining cause is not empirically warranted. It does not make any significant difference in our quest for causes of neurotic symptoms. Nor can such a hypothesis be empirically tested. Thus, we conclude that the hypothesis that repression could be the maintaining and not the originating cause is based upon an artificial distinction that is neither empirically nor rationally warranted. Therefore, failure to eliminate such a hypothesis constitutes no violation of the rules of causal inference.

Section III

Elimination of rival hypotheses

We now come to the consideration of part (ii) of Grünbaum's objections against the repression argument; namely, that in arriving at repression aetiology Freud and Breuer had failed to eliminate the rival hypothesis of suggestion. This is by far a more serious objection. Can we eliminate the placebo hypothesis related to the cure with reasonable certainty? My reply to this objection will not be based on the historical evidence on which Grünbaum has based Freud's repression argument. I shall deal with the general problem: is it possible to formulate a logically acceptable argument for the repression aetiology on the basis of clinical evidence? Before discussing this problem, we have to know that Grünbaum means the following by a placebo hypothesis:

> A treatment modality T has a number of central features for a target disorder D. T also has a number of incidental features. If the therapeutic gains of T are causally related to the incidental features of T rather than the central features of T, then the therapeutic gain is said to be due to placebo factors.

In other words, any therapeutic gain in order to be genuine must be shown to be causally related to the central features of T. In order to achieve this, they must not be shown to be causally related to any incidental features of T.

It is to be noted that, according to Grünbaum, these incidental factors are called placebos only relative to a given treatment modality. It will be false to assume that they are in general devoid of causal effectiveness. Even the celebrated sugar pill, which is used as a placebo in so many clinical experiments, is not devoid of genuine therapeutic efficacy when administered in the case of hypoglycaemia. Nor are placebos devoid of the capacity to bring about very specific effects. A sugar pill is a placebo in relation to aspirin therapy. But taken in the belief that it is aspirin may bring about complete relief of the symptom. Hence, placebos are not in general causally ineffective agents.

According to Grünbaum's characterisation, a cure brought about by the suggestive influence of a therapist would not be a placebo effect for a primarily suggestive therapy. But a therapeutic gain related to suggestion in psychoanalytic therapy will be a placebo effect, because suggestions are not claimed to be the constituent features of psychoanalytic therapy. Thus, to substantiate the claim of therapeutic efficacy of a given treatment modality, Grünbaum says it is necessary to show that the treatment gains are not due to any incidental feature of T. After eliminating the incidental factors as the possible candidates for the therapeutic gain, it needs to be shown that the treatment gains are due to the central features of the therapy. This latter task is to be achieved by showing that the treatment gains were invariably present when the therapy was administered and there was no counter-instance.

A therapy may be in general a placebo therapy. This would be the case when the constituent features of a therapy fail to be therapeutic for a target disorder D. In other words, the therapeutic gains of a placebo therapy, if any, are causally related to the incidental rather than to the characteristic features of the therapy. A therapy may be in general a non-placebo therapy, but some of its effects may be due to incidental features. In all such cases, those specific effects would be considered placebo effects precisely because they have been wrought by the incidental features. We can now define the placebo effect of a therapy as per Grünbaum:

> G is a placebo effect of a treatment modality T if and only if there are features a, b, c, that are incidental features of T and G is causally related to a, b, c.

A placebo hypothesis, therefore, is a hypothesis that attributes causal relevance for a therapeutic gain to the incidental features of a treatment modality. If we accept this then the incidental features of a therapy become rival causal candidates and should be eliminated like other causal candidates that may not form constituent parts of the therapy.

Applied in the context of psychoanalysis, the most important placebo hypothesis is the hypothesis regarding the suggestive influence of the therapist. This is an incidental feature of the psychoanalytic therapy. Its characteristic feature is insight, or as Grünbaum would have it, lifting of repression. Thus, in order to substantiate the claim that the therapeutic gains are due to the characteristic features of the psychoanalytic therapy, the following two claims have to be shown to be true:

(i) There is a causal relation between the characteristic feature of the psychoanalytic therapy and the therapeutic gain.
(ii) The treatment gain is not due to the suggestive influence of the therapist.

The second point is the problem of elimination of the placebo hypothesis. It is our task to show that it is possible within a clinical situation to arrive at a reasonably certain conclusion that the cures are not due to suggestion.

Before we start answering this question, a little clarification of the above account is needed. Grünbaum's view about the placebo effect is not in consonance with our commonly accepted view of placebos.

Our common concept of placebos is that they are causally impotent. To ascribe to them causal effectiveness seems inconsistent. Drug placebos are those that are found to be chemically inert; for example, the celebrated sugar pill. This deprives them of the capacity to bring about a change in the bodily condition by bringing about a change in the chemical state of the body. This is why they are considered neither harmful nor beneficial, and devoid of *real* causal potency in most cases. The latter assertion is based upon the assumption that only chemical changes present in the drug have causal potency to bring about changes in the chemical state of the body. This assumption, however, cannot be supported by evidence. Placebos have been found to produce chemical changes in the body. For example:

> McRae et al. (2004) demonstrated that sham surgery for stem-cell replacement in Parkinson's disease yielded potent and long-lived placebo responses. Further implicating the importance of dopamine in placebo responses Benedetti et al. (2003) recently demonstrated that the rate and pattern of neuronal activation in subthalamic nuclei is modified by placebo in a manner that mimics dopaminergic stimulation. (Kradin, 2008, pp. 167–168)

We are then faced with the apparent inconsistency that a chemical change has been brought about by a chemically inert substance. One way to solve this difficulty would be to adopt the following principle: a placebo brings about the same results as a genuine therapy by initiating a causal chain different from the one stimulated by the genuine therapy. Thus, aspirin therapy for headaches brings about relief by initiating a chain of chemical reactions in the body. A placebo of sugar pill arouses a chain of psychological reactions, which, in turn, brings about the same results as those of the aspirin therapy.

This, however, does not solve the problem. Placebos are still considered causal agents, having causal potency. If the causal chain through which they brought about the therapeutic result is different from the one associated with a genuine therapy for a disorder, this provides us with no reason to call them causally impotent. In this respect they are equivalent to an alternative therapy of the same disorder. Drug X and drug Y both may be able to bring about remission of a disorder D by initiating two completely different causal chains. But neither of them is a placebo in the sense of being causally impotent.

Grünbaum's approach that each is a placebo in the context of the other also does not seem acceptable. To call a therapeutically active drug a placebo does not seem to fit our common notion of placebos. The word "placebo" has acquired a derogatory emotive connotation. To call a chemically potent drug having curative power in specified diseases a "placebo" gives rise to confusion as well as to a not too favourable psychological reaction towards the drug in question. Just imagine calling penicillin a placebo because it was an incidental feature in the treatment of the common cold. I, therefore, propose that the concept of placebo be given up. The placebos should be considered genuine causal candidates and be eliminated just as other rival causal candidates are eliminated. Since incidental therapeutic features have to be eliminated anyway—placebos or not—it is much better to consider them as rival causal candidates.

Even in experimental clinical trials, it is not necessary to call the sugar pill a placebo. Instead we may simply compare the results of, say, aspirin therapy with the results of sugar pill therapy. This proposition does not bring about any substantial change in the area of medical testing; it merely tries to get rid of a confusing concept. Henceforth, I shall call the placebo hypothesis in relation to the repression aetiology the specific name of "the suggestion hypothesis".

There are two rival causal candidates for a cure claimed to be effected by a psychoanalytic therapy; (a) spontaneous remission, and (b) suggestion. Both of these are formidable rivals and it is important to eliminate them as possible causal candidates before the characteristic features of the therapy can be causally linked with the cure.

To say that a symptom has cured spontaneously is not to say that the cure was uncaused but to say that it was causally unrelated to the therapy in question. Grünbaum's favourite example is that of drinking coffee and curing a cold. P is suffering from a cold and a friend advises him to drink coffee for a month, which, he assures P, would definitely cure the cold. P follows his friend's advice and his cold is cured in one month. P thanks his friend for giving such valuable advice. Yet we all know that P's drinking coffee has nothing to do with the cure of the cold. The cold had a spontaneous remission and the therapeutic efficacy was wrongly attributed to drinking coffee. Grünbaum says that unless we have a control group of cold sufferers with no coffee-drinking and another with coffee-drinking, it is not possible for us to determine whether drinking coffee is causally relevant for the cure of a cold. A similar situation is obtained in the clinical sessions of psychoanalysis.

Unless we have control and experimental groups—the control group without any psychotherapy and the experimental group undergoing therapy—and are able to compare the rate of remission, any conclusion regarding the efficacy of the therapy is not justified.

The question of spontaneous remission has been a major source of worry for psychotherapists since 1952, when Eysenck pronounced, on the basis of statistical interpretation of some data, that the rate of remission by psychotherapy is no greater than that of spontaneous remission. This put the credibility of all psychotherapies in question. However, Eysenck's interpretation of data has been severely criticised, most notably by Bergin in 1971, who reanalysed Eysenck's data and pointed out some major problems including a "multitude of arithmetical error, misinterpretation of original data, non-comparable comparison groups", etc. (McNeilly & Howard, 1991, p. 74).

In a new re-evaluation, McNeilly and Howard subjected the data used by Eysenck to probit analysis with regards to "variations in the amount of therapy received" and came up with the following surprise results:

> Treatment was associated with significantly higher rates of improvement when compared to the effects of spontaneous remission. In fact, 50% of psychotherapy patients were estimated to improve after 8 weeks, whereas only 2% of the untreated patients were estimated to improve in this time. Probit analysis showed that the 50% improvement rate for Eysenck's spontaneous remission group occurred at a much later time than the 50% improvement rate for psychotherapy. According to his % improvement estimates, psychotherapy accomplishes in about 15 sessions what spontaneous remission takes two years to do. Thus, Eysenck's data show that psychotherapy is very effective. (McNeilly & Howard, 1991, p. 74)

The authors conclude by saying:

> Perhaps we can now concentrate our attention elsewhere having shown that Eysenck's evaluation actually revealed that psychotherapy is quite effective. (Ibid., 1991, p. 78)

However, in any individual case it remains to be shown that the cure was not spontaneous but was causally related to the therapy in question. In some cases we are able to arrive at causal conclusions with reasonable certainty even without the use of a control and experimental group. This requires very specific knowledge of causal processes involved in bringing about a given effect and taking into account specific characteristics of the effect. For example, in most cases we are able to determine whether a particular fire was caused by an electric short circuit or a lighted match thrown on a pile of papers. We are able to determine whether a given poisoning death is due to arsenic or due to cyanide. In all these cases the effect has been specialised (see Pap, 1962). One is not investigating the cause of a fire only, but fire of a given sort. One is not investigating the cause of a death only, but death of a given kind. The effect has certain characteristic features and can be explained with the help of the causal processes involved in bringing them about. The more our knowledge progresses with regards to these causal processes the greater is the certainty in these cases. Probably Wesley Salmon would consider these as cases of causal processes leaving their mark.

If spontaneous remissions have such characteristic features they can be used to eliminate the rival hypothesis. The important question in this respect is: do we have such specific knowledge about the characteristic features of spontaneous remission and the causal processes involved therein? There have not been too many systematic investigations done to isolate the factors that are causally related to spontaneous remission. However, there are some studies that provide us with a glimpse of the mental processes at work in cases of spontaneous remission. I give below the results of a German study:

> The findings suggest that: (1) Clinical symptoms go into remission more easily than do intrapsychic states; (2) the accumulation of psychic crisis in the social network fosters processes of change, and (3) patients' means of self-help can be structurally comparable to professional strategies. (Schweitzer, 1984, pp. 249–256)

A corollary of (3) in the above quote is that the patient consciously tries to overcome her incapacity and invents processes to overcome them. This is a conscious voluntary activity and a report from the subject should be able to give us the relevant information regarding it.

The rate of improvement in spontaneous remission is much slower than in psychotherapy. Thus, a symptom takes much less time to disappear when the patient undergoes psychotherapy and follows the instructions of the therapist. Almost always spontaneous remissions occur gradually. It does not happen that one fine morning a person gets up from bed and finds his or her symptoms gone. Therefore, the disappearance of a symptom soon after a therapeutic process aimed at alleviating it need not be attributed to spontaneous remission. Thus, Anna O.'s famous aversion to drinking water disappeared immediately after she recalled the event with which it had originated; namely, her experience of seeing a dog lapping water from a glass and her resulting anger and disgust. This remission is less likely to be a spontaneous cure. With the recollection of the relevant event, the patient was able to identify and face her anger and disgust. This insight occurred simultaneously with the recollection of the event. In spontaneous remission this would have taken a much longer course.

There are different rates of remission for different kinds of neuroses. There is no evidence that severe neuroses have a high rate of spontaneous remission. Chances are that the rate of remission in severe personality disorders, acute anxiety, acute depression, primary enuresis or severe obsession-compulsion disorder is comparatively low, while mild depression and mild obsession-compulsion have higher rates of spontaneous remission. A therapist may also isolate external factors that may have been causally connected with the remission of the symptoms. Suppose a patient has expressed deep anxiety related to her financial situation. Her anxiety significantly lessens soon after her financial condition improves. Chances are the remission is due to this external factor. The therapist can take into account such factors and find out whether the remission was due to an external factor or to the processes related to the therapy.

With the help of these characteristic features it will be possible to eliminate the hypothesis of spontaneous remission in most cases though perhaps not in all cases. Insofar as the strategies employed by the patient are structurally the same as the professional ones, they do not speak against the efficacy of the therapy in question. If a therapist asks the patient to try to forcibly stop the obsessive thoughts and the patient had already been trying, the efforts of the patient are consonant with the therapy and do not constitute evidence against the therapy.

Now, we come to the rival hypothesis of suggestion. How do we know that the cure was not due to suggestion but due to the lifting of repression and so on? The analogy of coffee-drinking is relevant here also. It is possible that the entire process of analytic therapy is analogous to coffee-drinking, which is causally irrelevant to a cure, and it was the suggestions given by the therapist during the process of treatment that was responsible for cure.

The charge of suggestion has been haunting psychoanalysis since its birth. In my opinion its strength comes from our ignorance of exact processes involved in the effectiveness of suggestion and in its amorphousness. Various senses of "suggestion" are lumped together without any consideration as to whether they are relevant to the particular feature one is referring to in relation to the therapeutic effect. So, it is important to give this hypothesis a precise formulation in each case and eliminate them one by one. We also need to carefully state the resources that are at the disposal of the analyst in the clinical situation to discount these hypotheses. I shall discuss below the two main formulations of this hypothesis.

(1) The direct suggestions of the analyst are the cause of P's cure.
(2) The indirect subtle suggestions of the analyst created a false belief in P's mind, which ultimately caused his cure.

The resources that the analyst has at his or her disposal are the following:

- Some background knowledge about the effects of suggestion.
- The clinical data obtained during the sessions.

Let us take both these versions of this rival hypothesis and see whether the analyst can eliminate them. First, direct suggestions are not given in proper psychoanalytic treatment; therefore they are irrelevant to analytic therapy and do not need to be eliminated. Indirect suggestions of the analyst are a relevant candidate for placebo hypothesis relative to psychoanalytic therapy and very difficult to eliminate. It was P's belief in the truth of the interpretations of the analyst and not the truth of the interpretations themselves that was causally related to his cure. Thus, P is, in reality, cured by suggestion and not by insight or the lifting of the repression, as claimed by repression theorists.

- We can eliminate this hypothesis in the following ways: By showing that P's belief regarding the cause of his symptoms is irrelevant in the cure of his symptoms. But this course is not open to analysts, since the therapy is related to bringing about a change in P's belief structure.

- By showing that false beliefs about the causes of symptoms do not lead to cure of symptoms or at least to a durable cure of symptoms. We have some empirical evidence regarding this, but not enough to provide significant support to the conclusion.
- By showing that P's beliefs regarding the cause of his symptoms are true, which amounts to showing that the analytic therapy is causally connected with the cure.

Let us begin with a specific psychoanalytic hypothesis: repressed homosexuality is the cause of delusion. For the sake of simplicity, I refrain from mentioning the more complex hypothesis; namely, projection of repressed homosexuality is the cause of delusions. A lower level hypothesis derivable from this would be: P's repressed homosexuality is the cause of his delusions. It is this lower level hypothesis that can be tested within the analytical setting. Thus, if P suffers from delusions and comes for psychoanalytical treatment, we can investigate whether there is relevant evidence present in the clinical data to justify the causal connection between P's repressed homosexuality and his delusion, which will provide confirmatory evidence for the general hypothesis that repressed homosexuality is the cause of delusion by being its positive instance. According to Mill's criteria, such a causal inference requires the following two types of evidence for justification:

(a) Evidence related to the association of P's repressed homosexuality and his delusions.
(b) Evidence related to the association of the absence of P's repressed homosexuality and absence of his delusion.

The general hypothesis regarding the connection between repressed homosexuality and delusion would be confirmed if the causal inference expressed in it is based on the above two types of evidence. Is it possible to obtain this evidence in analytic sessions?

Let us suppose that during the course of treatment the patient gradually overcomes his resistance. Slowly he realises and admits in the course of treatment that each male he was suspicious of regarding his wife's affections, was one he himself admired and felt inferior to. On the contrary, men who he did not find sexually attractive he did not become jealous about. Often homosexual thoughts have come across his mind but he has always tried to banish them. As analysis progresses, he produces homosexual phantasies directed towards the men he had accused his wife of being attracted to. Suppose with the gradual release of repressed homosexuality his delusions also start lessening.

Since the data are granted to be valid, we can conclude that the analyst has evidence of the type (a). We still need evidence of the type (b). Let us suppose again that as the analysis progresses the patient slowly comes to terms with his own homosexuality and could at least enjoy homosexual phantasies without feeling guilty or inferior. In the course of analysis he brings up materials that if he meets a man whom he finds attractive he now is able to indulge in homosexual phantasies related to him. In the past, whenever he felt attracted towards a man, he had tried to banish the thought from his mind and subsequently had developed delusions towards him. But in similar circumstances he does not feel delusions any more.

A report of this type should be considered supportive evidence that it was repression of homosexuality and not merely homosexuality that was causally related to the formation of delusions. However, it is possible that the analyst subtly suggested to P that if he was able to accept his homosexuality, he would be cured of his delusion of jealousy. So, it was his belief in the verdict of psychoanalysis rather than the resolution of his repressed homosexuality that was causally connected with his cure.

Let us suppose the suggestion given by the analyst is true. Not all suggestions are false. I may suggest to my friend that her tendency to dominate everyone around her is causing people to dislike her. My suggestion may be true. My friend tried to modify her behaviour and got positive results. The cause of her being liked by others is her change of behaviour, not my suggestion. My suggestions worked as an instrument in bringing to her attention what the real causal factor was behind her problem. If, therefore, the suggestion of the analyst is true; namely, the repressed homosexuality of P was actually causally connected with his delusions of jealousy, no harm is done. Suggestion here has acted as an instrument in helping P realise the causal factor behind his symptoms.

Suppose that the suggestion is false. P does not have repressed homosexuality, yet he is experiencing homosexual phantasies, enjoying them and bringing about relevant emotions that he is experiencing now as a result of suggestions. This is the relevant sense in which suggestion is a rival candidate to understanding, insight, or behaviour modification, and so on. If this is the case, the data become contaminated by the suggestive influence of the analyst whereas we have already assumed that the data are free of contamination. Given the case, one cannot escape the conclusion that repression of homosexuality is causally connected with the symptoms of P.

It may be objected that the evidence I have supplied in support of repressed homosexuality and delusion being causally connected is too well formed. Such evidence is not generally obtainable in analytic settings. It is true that case histories are often not presented in this way. But it is possible to give them such formulation. As early as in *Studies on Hysteria*, in the case of Elizabeth Von R., Freud cited such evidence. As the conflict related to her symptoms was getting resolved, her symptoms started subsiding. They re-emerged as the conflict re-emerged.

A further objection may be that the evidence that I have cited is completely based on the introspective report of the subject. It is the subject who supplies how he feels regarding other males. It is the subject again who reports that he now indulges in homosexual phantasies, etc. These are unreliable data and provide little support to the causal inference. To this, it may be replied that in the present context we are not concerned with the validity of data but with the justification of causal inference. If the data were granted to be valid, then the inference is justified. Whether the data are truly valid or not is a matter related to the reliability of evidence—a problem I have discussed at length in previous chapters. Even then a few words will not be out of place here.

Though the controversy surrounding the reliability of introspective reports is too great to be ignored, it is worth mentioning that most of this controversy is related to causal connections arrived at by the introspectionist on the basis of his own awareness of his own psychological states. Most psychologists agree that reports consisting of the contents of one's own psychological states are mostly free from errors. Even Nisbett and Wilson, who are not supporters of introspection, say:

> An important source of belief in introspective awareness is undoubtedly related to the fact that we do indeed have direct access to a great storehouse of private knowledge. Jones and Nisbett (1972) have enumerated a list of types of privately held knowledge that bears repeating in the present context. The individual knows a host of personal historical facts: he knows the focus of his attention at any given point in time; he knows what his current sensations are and has what all psychologists and philosophers would assert to

> be "knowledge" at least quantitatively superior to that of observers concerning his emotions, and plans. (Nisbett & Wilson, 1977)

Thus, in so far as we can limit the introspection to reporting the contents of any given psychological state, the chances of error are very little. In the example I have given above the clinical evidence is limited to the report of the content of P's psychological states. None of the reports that have been utilised in arriving at the causal inference are based on the patient's reports of causal connections between his own mental states.

There are other difficulties also. Does the analytic session have a setting powerful enough to bring about intense emotional experiences in P when the relevant psychological states are not present in P's mind? Bringing about such strong emotional states and uncritical compliance to suggestion is characteristic of a hypnotic state. It is possible to bring such changes by direct suggestion in the state of hypnosis. Even then the changes will be short-lived. Modern research has indicated that emotions brought about by suggestions in the laboratories have been later recalled as being "suggested" and had no influence on the real life of the subject (See Fromm & Shire, 1979). We have to remember that in analytic sessions P is not hypnotised; he is not in a totally passive and uncritical state of mind. He retains his rationality, and in spite of his psychological dependence on the analyst he is not passively compliant in every respect, which is the case in hypnotic inductions. Therefore, continuously bringing about intense emotional experiences and working through them, which is the characteristic process of analytic therapy, is very difficult to explain unless we suppose that these psychological materials genuinely belong to P and are not due to any external force like suggestion.

It is often said that indirect suggestion works without letting the person know that he is being influenced and hence is more powerful than direct suggestion. Experimental studies suggest otherwise. In a well-controlled study on the effectiveness of direct and indirect suggestion the results show:

> The indirect suggestion resulted in greater compliance in the hypnotic condition, and direct suggestions resulted in greater compliance in non-hypnotic condition. Susceptibility to hypnosis was related to compliance in the hypnosis condition, but no interactions were found between susceptibility and types of suggestion. (Stone, 1985, pp. 256–263)

In another very well controlled study on the effect of wording in hypnotic responding and induction, it was found that:

> Subjects experienced suggestion-related involuntariness and suggested effects to a greater degree in response to direct-worded suggestion than in indirect-worded suggestion. (Lynn, Neufeld, & Matyi, 1987, pp. 76–79)

These studies indicate that the power of direct suggestion is much stronger than the power of indirect suggestion. In the study by Lynn, Neufeld and Matyi direct wording was characterised as "authoritative language, specific responses" and indirect wording was characterised as "permissive language, choice of responses". Direct authoritative suggestions have been found more effective in bringing about the desired response. And we know even these responses are not durable. They require repeated inductions.

Thus, the analytic setting is totally inadequate to bring about the kind of emotional responses exhibited by P, above, working through them with the help of indirect suggestion. Also, if the emotional experiences are not at all related to the content of P's mind but have been induced, they need to be constantly strengthened by suggestions and require a continued state of suggestibility on the part of the analysand. If it is found that the treatment gains are lasting even after P's state of suggestibility or after his dependence on the analyst is over, there is reason to believe that the belief change was related to the real content of mind rather than to an externally inducted suggestion.

As far as the nature of cure is concerned, the cure brought about by an unearthing of repression and consequent correction of attitude will be qualitatively superior to one brought about by suggestion. The former will be more durable, far more encompassing, and capable of being extended to other related fields, whereas the latter will be narrow in scope. One can very easily explain the difference by the causal processes involved in bringing about these changes. I conclude, therefore, that it is possible to eliminate the rival causal hypotheses mentioned by Grünbaum in arriving at repression aetiology. This is a weaker claim but I have shown that it can be done in a plausible way. This removes the logical obstruction in the valid formulation of the repression aetiology.

Note

1. I am thankful to Prof. Adolf Grünbaum for supplying me with the Hirschmüller reference.

CHAPTER SIX

Causal fallacies in psychoanalysis

In the previous chapter, I was concerned with showing how the objections related to the valid formulation of repression aetiology can be overcome. The problem of valid causal inference is not merely related to the repression aetiology. It is related to the very process of intra-clinical testing itself. The problem is especially acute in the case of testing psychoanalytic hypotheses. Grünbaum has claimed that even though data from individual sessions can be scrutinised and may be found acceptable, no statistical generalisation of a psychoanalytic hypothesis can be accepted on the basis of clinical material (see Grünbaum, 1988, pp. 623–658). In *Foundations* itself, Grünbaum has taken a more rigid stance. He has denied the possibility of any kind of reliable testing on the bases of clinical data. He further claims that causal inferences psychoanalysts derive from clinical materials are fraught with serious logical fallacies and are simply logically unacceptable. In this chapter, I shall deal with some of his objections related to the fallacious causal inferences in the clinical setting.

Section I

Errors in causal inferences

One important error related to causal inferences is to derive causal inferences without the appropriate negative instances. This has been an important source of error in clinical settings, according to Grünbaum. This basic rule of inference has been repeatedly violated by psychoanalysts in their clinical settings. The reason is that the clinical setting simply does not have the resources to provide negative evidence for a causal generalisation. Testing of a hypothesis could be either retrospective or prospective. A retrospective statistical testing of a hypothesis is commonly known as a case control study. In this kind of study, a causal relation between two properties is tested after the hypothesised effect has taken place. For example, in order to retrospectively test the causal relation between smoking and lung cancer, smoking habits of patients suffering from lung cancer are compared with a control group. The reliability of retrospective studies is considered less than that of prospective studies. A clinical testing of psychoanalytical hypotheses, however, will always be retrospective because in all such cases the effect—namely, the symptom—has already occurred.

Suppose, Grünbaum says, in a retrospective study the general causal statement to be justified is the following: all Ns are Ps. Let N stand for neurotic and P for people having the required kind of repressed experiences. The justification of this statement not only requires evidence that all cases of Ns be cases of Ps, it also requires that all non-Ps are non-Ns. According to Mill's criterion, without the support of negative causal inference "all non-Ps are non-Ns" the positive causal inference "all Ns are Ps" is not justified. It may be said that both the positive and negative causal inferences are logically equivalent; hence any evidence that supports negative causal inference will provide support to the positive causal inference "all Ns are Ps" also. But this logical equivalence does not solve the problem of causal justification. Grünbaum says that the issue is not of logical equivalence here. The issue is to provide evidential support for the strong causal relevance claimed in the hypothesis. For this it is necessary to show that there are cases of non-Ps who are non-Ns also (*Foundations*, p. 254).

The clinical setting at best can provide evidence for "All Ns are Ps", but not for "All non-Ps are non-Ns." The latter is essential to show that being a P makes a difference in being an N. Grünbaum emphasises that since Freud considers repression a necessary condition for neuroses, the class of people who do not have the required kind of repression must not contain a single case of a neurotic, while the population having the required kind of repressed experience must have a large, though numerically unspecifiable, number of neurotics.

One way of acquiring negative instances for "All Ns are Ps" within the clinical situation is to consider the class of patients who are suffering from some form of neurosis other than the neurosis whose specific aetiology is in question, say, obsession neurosis. Grünbaum says: let us call these people non-Ns. We will then have two possible cases:

(i) All non-Ns are Ps. In other words, these "non-neurotic" people do have the required kind of repressed experiences. But this inference does not provide support to "all Ns are Ps", because this is compatible with "all non-Ns are Ps". It does not require them, though it requires "all non-Ps are non-Ns".
(ii) All non-Ns are non-Ps: also fails to provide support to "all Ns are Ps". Because together with the evidence that "All Ns are Ps" it merely shows that within the class of neurotics "All Ns are Ps". It does not show that within the larger class of normal people, being a P is causally relevant to being an N.

This is insufficient evidence for a causal connection, because if the general population is taken into account, the hypothesised causal factor may turn out to be merely accidental. So, Grünbaum says that the clinical setting simply does not have the epistemic resources that could provide evidence that P (a person having the required kind of repressed experience) is neurosogenic (*Foundations*, p. 258).

There are two ways to handle this problem. My first approach refers to what an inductive generalisation claims. The following solution has often been suggested for the Raven paradox. Consider the two claims:

(a) All ravens are black.
(b) Almost all ravens are black.
    (a′) All non-black things are non-ravens.
    (b′) Almost all non-black things are non-ravens.

While (a) is equivalent to (a′), (b′) is not equivalent to (b). In fact, (b′) has no bearing on the confirmation of (b). It is completely independent of (b). There is a weakening of claim from (a) to (b). But this is not considered detrimental to an inductive generalisation. In fact, one may emphasise that inductive generalisations are weaker generalisations and need not fulfil the strict deductive criterion of a universal proposition.

If so, one may weaken the claim of psychoanalytic propositions. It will be sufficient to claim that *almost all* neuroses are caused by repressed conflict instead of claiming that *all* neuroses are caused by repressed conflict. In such a case, there would be no need to show that almost all non-Ps are non-Ns, because the latter is simply not related to the former claim. It provides no confirmatory evidence for the former. This would imply that only instances that satisfy the antecedent and consequent of a hypothesis would be confirmatory of a given hypothesis. An instance that satisfies the antecedent but not the consequent would be a negative instance. The same may apply in the case of psychoanalytic hypotheses also. Cases of neuroses satisfying both the antecedent and consequent would be confirmatory to the repression hypothesis. Cases of neuroses that are not cases of repressed conflict would be its disconfirming evidence. The entire class of non-P, which is non-N, becomes simply independent of the claims made in the repression hypothesis.

Grünbaum may, however, object to this approach. He has formulated the psychoanalytic hypotheses as universal causal hypotheses where "universal" is taken to mean unrestricted universal hypotheses. This formulation of the causal hypothesis "all Ns are Ps" as "almost all Ns are Ps" may not be acceptable to him. This will lead us to the second approach.

It should be recognised that Grünbaum's objection that other patients who are not suffering from the disease under investigation cannot provide negative evidence for a hypothesis of the form "all Ns are Ps" is related to the external validity of a statistical generalisation. It is related essentially to the question: under what circumstances can the results of a study done on a sample group be extended beyond that group? The validity of such a generalisation depends on how representative the sample is of the population on which the study is being conducted. Since most of the studies are related to general population, one of the conditions of the validity of statistical generalisation is that the sample on which the study has been conducted must be representative of the general population. The normal procedure to achieve such representative sampling is through random selection of the group on which the study is being conducted. Any other method of selection compromises the representativeness of the sample by introducing selection bias and thus makes the generalisation invalid. In the example that Grünbaum has described, if a control group is formed with patients suffering from neuroses other than the one being investigated, the group will not be a representative of the general population. The results of the study, therefore, will not be generalisable to the normal population at large.

However, in statistical studies representative sampling is more of a theoretical ideal than a goal achieved in practice. Prof. Henry Kyburg, Jr once remarked to me jokingly that only laboratory rats can be selected randomly. In practice, a study group is rarely selected by a random process. Scientific studies are nevertheless conducted by applying appropriate statistical measures to take care of the errors resulting from selection bias. Careful consideration is also given to interpreting the results of such studies. In fact, in epidemiology the most common method used in forming control groups in retrospective studies is to select patients admitted in the same or other hospitals who don't have the disease under investigation. I quote:

> The method most commonly used in conducting retrospective studies is to select the cases from one or more hospitals. Almost all retrospective studies of the association between cigarette smoking and lung cancer have used this method. The control groups usually consist of patients with *other diseases* in the same hospital. This method is popular because the data can generally be obtained quickly, easily, and inexpensively, but several assumptions and sources of bias must be considered in evaluating the findings from such studies. (my emphasis) (Lilienfeld & Lilienfeld, 1980, p. 169)

If we accept Grünbaum's argument, then these studies prove that only within the class of sick persons smoking makes a difference in the occurrence of cancer. These results are not generalisable to the general population because the class of sick people is not representative of the general population. But as I have pointed out, it is simply incorrect to say that such studies are methodologically flawed under all circumstances. They do lead to biased results if care is not taken in the formation of study groups to minimise selection bias and to adopt appropriate statistical measures that have been devised to improve the reliability of such studies. An account of these statistical procedures can be found in any introductory epidemiology textbook. As Rothman notes:

> Some textbooks have stressed the need for representativeness in the selection of cases and controls; the advice has been that cases are supposed to be representative of all persons with the disease and

> that controls should be representative of the entire non diseased population. Such advice is clearly wrong.
>
> A case-control study may be restricted to any type of case that may be of interest: female cases, old cases, severely ill cases, case that died soon after disease onset, mild cases … and so on. In none of these examples would the cases be representative of all persons with the disease, and yet perfectly valid case-control studies are possible using such unrepresentative case series …
>
> It is entirely wrong to seek controls that are representative of the entire non-diseased population. The main objective in selecting controls is to select subjects who represent those who might have become cases on the study: if cases are selected from one hospital out of many in a city, the control should represent those people who, had they developed the disease under study, would have gone to the same hospital. (Rothman, 1986, pp. 64–65)

The fact is that retrospective studies are done regularly in epidemiology by forming control groups consisting of patients not suffering from the diseases under investigation, but from other diseases. The situation is relevantly similar to the one described by Grünbaum in the case of psychoanalytic studies. One may wonder why the strategy cannot be applied in the case of psychoanalytic retrospective designs.

Grünbaum is also wrong in saying that analysts do not have a normal population to form control groups. People coming for training in psychoanalysis are essentially normal. In fact, within my knowledge, at least some psychoanalytic institutes (mine being one of them) have the rule that persons showing manifest symptoms are not allowed to be training candidates. Also, some people come for analysis just to know themselves. This population may be utilised for the purpose of forming control groups in retrospective studies. Any such study, however, would introduce selection bias. But one may adopt statistical measures similar to those recommended in epidemiological retrospective studies to counteract these various biases.

Generalisation on the basis of retrospective studies should be attempted with caution. As more and more studies are replicated with different population groups, the results of the studies can be made more reliable and more generalisable. From this point of view psychoanalysis has a very desirable population group. Psychoanalytic institutes are spread worldwide. Thus, people from widely varied cultural, geographical and environmental backgrounds come to be treated by psychoanalytic therapy. This may take care of some part of the bias introduced by the self-selection of people in the groups of Ns.

Grünbaum may have two possible objections against this procedure. First, statistical measures that are applied to improve the reliability of retrospective epidemiological studies are difficult to apply in psychoanalytic contexts. Hence, the point that such studies are reliably done in epidemiology is irrelevant in the context of psychoanalytic hypotheses-testing. But this objection is far from being a methodological one. It may not even be true. For example, one of the methods suggested to counteract selection bias in epidemiological retrospective studies is not to select patients from the same hospital or being treated by one doctor. Groups should be formed by selecting patients from different doctors and hospitals. It is also commonly agreed that the reliability of the results of a retrospective study increases if other retrospective studies done on different population groups support the result.

There seems to be no difficulty in applying these measures to retrospective psychoanalytic studies too. Studies done with different patient groups formed on the basis of proper statistical measures should provide some support to causal inferences in the case of psychoanalytic studies also, as they do in epidemiological studies.

The second objection Grünbaum may have is: psychoanalytic retrospective studies may need special statistical measures other than those used in epidemiological studies. Such a programme has not been worked out yet. For one thing, it is not certain that some special statistical measures may be required for conducting retrospective studies in psychoanalysis along the lines of those conducted in epidemiology. But if they do, the problem is not a methodological one. There is no reason to believe that such a programme cannot be worked out, since the proposition is fairly plausible. I conclude, therefore, that this objection of Grünbaum's can be taken care of and is not essentially a methodological one.

Insufficient and inadequate evidence

Psychoanalytic case studies, according to Grünbaum, are replete with causal inferences drawn on insufficient and inadequate evidence and are fraught with logical fallacies. This is especially true in the case of some causal inferences peculiarly related to psychoanalytic hypotheses.

One of these is deriving causal inferences on the basis of transference phenomenon. Let us call this the transference fallacy. A transference phenomenon is characterised by a strong emotional attitude of the patient towards his analyst. The psychoanalytic explanation of this phenomenon is that the repressed childhood emotions of the patient related to significant figures in his life are mobilised towards the analyst. Thus, in the transference the patient is recapitulating his repressed childhood conflicts and experiences. This transfer of an emotional attitude could be positive or negative, depending upon the emotions transferred. The analyst often utilises the transference phenomenon to hypothesise regarding the early childhood conflicts of the patient.

Most aetiological hypotheses in psychoanalysis are related to early childhood experiences. Grünbaum says that either these memories are extremely unreliable or are not reproduced in the analytic sessions at all. The psychoanalyst, however, derives causal inferences by reconstructing the childhood experiences on the basis of transference and gives interpretations to his patients. Such causal inferences are unjustified for several reasons. In his paper, "The role of the case study method in the foundation of psychoanalysis" (1988), Grünbaum says that this kind of reasoning involves many logical fallacies, including the fallacy of begging the question. I briefly relate Grünbaum's objections below:

> Let us suppose that the hypothesis being tested is the following: P's repressed early childhood experience of a threatening father is causally related with her aversion to men. (I am overlooking the question whether the behaviour of P's father was actually threatening or whether P merely experienced it as threatening.)

Let us call the hypothesised cause C and the hypothesised effect E. Justification of the hypothesis stated above requires the following kind of evidence according to Grünbaum:

- P's veridical memory or independent evidence that C had actually occurred. P has actually experienced her father to be threatening.
- Evidence of a causal relation between this childhood experience and aversion to men. This evidence has to be of the following kind: (i) rival candidates for C must be eliminated, and (ii) C and E must have agreement in presence and absence.

In the course of analysis, P develops a strong emotional attitude towards her analyst in which she perceives him to be threatening. The analyst cites this as the evidence for P's repressed early childhood experience of a threatening father. But, according to Grünbaum, this reasoning is fallacious for the following reasons:

- It begs the aetiologic question that the emotional attitudes and conflicts that P experiences in relation to the analyst are causally related with the symptoms of P. Even if we grant the hypothesis that an earlier conflict has been revived in the analytic situation, it does not prove that the original conflict was causally related to the patient's symptoms.
- Similarly, no conflict focused on the doctor can be cogent evidence for any hypothesised childhood event as the pathogen of an illness.

Grünbaum says:

> ... No matter how strongly recapitulatory, how can phantasies focused on the doctor be cogent evidence that a hypothesized or vividly remembered infantile prototype (or simulacrum) of the conflict had been the crucial *original pathogen* ...? (Grünbaum, 1988, p. 651)

Put simply, Grünbaum's objection is that any behaviour that P directs towards her doctor is irrelevant as an evidence for a repressed early childhood experience of a threatening father. It is simply fallacious to cite any attitude directed towards the doctor as evidence that a similar childhood attitude is causally related with the symptoms.

It seems to me that Grünbaum's objection rests on the following grounds: to justify a causal inference of the form "C is causally relevant for E" one must have direct evidence that C is correlated both in presence and in absence with E or that the presence of C increases the probability of E. Consequently, even if one grants that the conflict directed towards the analyst is the revival of an earlier childhood conflict, this does not prove that the earlier conflict itself is causally related with the symptom of P.

Grünbaum further objects that the reasoning is circular because the psychoanalyst reasons that the transference emotions are pathogenic, since they are transfers of earlier childhood conflicts onto the analyst and earlier childhood conflicts are pathogenic. But it is precisely the latter part of the hypothesis that needs to be proved. Thus, without independent evidence that the childhood conflicts are pathogenic, the reasoning becomes circular. Hence, to avoid circular reasoning one must have independent evidence that the childhood conflicts are pathogenic. This objection is essentially the same as the previous one. Both the objections emphasise that independent evidence is required to prove that the original childhood conflicts are pathogenic.

Grünbaum is perfectly justified in saying that the emotions directed towards the analyst by themselves provide no evidence that an original conflict of the same type is causally related with P's symptoms. Neither does psychoanalysis claim so. We have to take a more careful look in order to clarify what really is happening in the transference situation. Before I take up this task, I would like to point out that not all inferences regarding the causal significance of childhood conflicts in the analytic setting are based on transference. Quite often independent evidence is available in the clinical setting regarding earlier original conflicts. However, I shall take Grünbaum's objection as applicable to those cases where such evidence is not available and the analyst derives a causal inference regarding the pathogenic nature of earlier childhood conflicts on the basis of transference.

Grünbaum's objection rests on one main ground: causal inference is not justified without direct evidence for such a relation between the two hypothesised properties. If we accept this strict criterion, it is almost impossible to justify such a causal inference as the one Grünbaum has mentioned. But are all our causal inferences justified by direct evidence? Many causal inferences are justified on the basis of indirect evidence. This is not to deny that inferences based on direct evidence are better justified or are more reliable, whereas inferences based on indirect evidence are less reliable but they are not necessarily fallacious. Consider the following instances:

Astronomers in Alpha Centauri were puzzled by a slight anomaly in the precession of one of their moons. They hypothesised the existence of an undiscovered planet as the cause of this anomaly. The planet could not be detected even with the help of the most powerful telescope they could build. However, to test the hypothesis, astronomers predicted the future positions of a number of planets based on the hypothesis that an undiscovered planet is exerting a force on these planets. They had gathered sufficient data to enable them to make such predictions. These predictions came out true. The causal hypothesis is indirectly supported. The actual detection of the planet would have conclusively verified the causal hypothesis, but the inference based on predictions supports the hypothesis to a great degree provided other rival explanations have been eliminated. Under these circumstances we cannot say that the causal inference is fallacious. This inference would gain more and more evidential support if more and more predictions based on the hypothesis came out true even if no one could ever see the undiscovered planet. A similar circumstance led to the discovery of the planet Neptune, though Neptune could be located and the hypothesis related to the discovery of Neptune could be conclusively verified.

A similar strategy could be adopted in the case of psychoanalysis also. The psychoanalyst is well aware of the transference phenomenon. He proceeds with the hypothesis that early emotional experiences of a patient related to significant persons in her life are transferred onto the analyst in the course of treatment. Suppose during the course of treatment P develops strong hostile feelings towards the analyst and starts perceiving him as threatening. The feeling of hatred is intense and completely unwarranted under the neutral setting of analysis. The analyst concludes that P's hostile feelings towards her analyst are a transference phenomenon and are a prototype of her early childhood attitude towards a significant person in her life; most probably a father figure. The analyst needs to test this hypothesis. He then formulates the following therapeutic assumption:

> If P's attitude towards her father is causally related with her symptoms, and P's attitude towards her analyst is a prototype of her early attitude towards her father, then the correction of her attitude towards her father should lead to the resolution of P's symptoms. The analyst will utilise P's attitude towards him in bringing up the relevant thoughts, memories, conflicts and emotions related to her father.

It is to be noted that the direction of treatment is not centring round P's attitude towards the analyst. But it is expected that P's attitude towards the analyst would bring the relevant emotional material to the fore. Thus, in the treatment work, causal inference is not based on P's feelings/emotions towards the analyst, but the actual therapeutic work is done on the psychic material that is stirred up and brought to the conscious level through the medium of the analyst's person. It is like pulling up a bucket full of water with the help of a rope. The rope is only the instrument needed to hold the bucket deep in the well and then pull it up. It can be safely discarded after the job is done.

However, analogy is not proof. I will cite a number of examples to show that actual psychological work is done on the psychic materials related to the original person whose emotions have been transferred onto the analyst. By this I am trying to show that the actual feelings worked on belong to the significant person in P's life and the psychological working through of these feelings leads to therapeutic gain, and that those actual feelings were pathogenic. I give below snippets from actual case materials. I quote three examples from the case materials of Ralph R. Greenson, the famous psychoanalyst.

Example 1

The patient, a young lady, came to the session in the evening due to a change of schedule. It was dark outside and the lights in the chamber of the analyst were on. The patient's demeanour was quiet and serene.

> The patient remains quiet and I am more and more struck by the glow of pleasure she seems silently to reflect. I say to her after some twenty minutes: "this hour seems different. What are you enjoying so silently and all to yourself?" She replies in a soft and dreamy voice: "I am lying here drinking in the peaceful feeling of this office. It is a haven. I am breathing in the fragrance of your cigar, I imagine you sitting in your big chair, puffing away comfortably and thoughtfully. Your voice sounds like coffee and rich cigar smoke, warm and cheering. I feel protected, safe, looked after. It seems like it's after midnight and everyone at home is asleep except my father and me. He is working in his study and I can smell his cigar and I can hear him making himself coffee. I used to wish I could creep into the room and curl up alongside of him. I would try to and would promise to keep as silent as a mouse, but he always brought me back to bed." (Greenson, 1967, p. 306)

Example 2

A male patient of Greenson's who was struggling for a long time to express his anger towards the analyst finally decided to express his feeling as if in a drunken state. He became verbally abusive, banged his fist on the wall, punched the couch, and finally jumped off the couch and came over to the chair of the analyst.

> He comes over to my chair and stands over me, shaking his finger at me and saying, "Who the hell do you think you are anyway?" I say nothing. But as he was about to stomp out of the office, I call out to him: "How does it feel to finally tell Pappa he's not so great after all?" The patient stops still in his tracks at the word Pappa. He turns around and looks at me. Slowly his angry features relax; he shakes his head; he walks slowly back to the couch, and sits down. Then he says slowly: "Well, I finally did it, finally, finally, finally, after all these years. I told you all off, you and my old man, and my big brother, all of you. I finally feel I'm a grown man and not just a little boy masquerading as a man." Then tears streamed down his cheeks. (Greenson, 1967, pp. 328–329)

Example 3

A woman patient of Greenson who was in her third year of analysis suddenly developed resistance in coming to the session because she felt there was an ominous quality in her analyst. When asked to clarify this "ominous quality":

> She goes on to depict a man who seems manly and active but who is actually feminine and passive. He is so passive that he would let his women patients slowly bleed to death without lifting a finger. The moment the patient says, "bleed to death" she gasps: "Oh my God! I know what that is—that's my father. I am mixing you up with my father" The patient is referring to an incident in childhood when, at age four, she discovered she was bleeding from the vagina and ran to her father, in a panic. He tried to comfort her by saying, "It's nothing, it will go away, forget about it." For many complicated reasons this was most disturbing to my patient. (Greenson, 1967, pp. 309–310)

These long quotations are aimed at showing that in transference feelings towards the analyst are traced back to their origin and the real psychological work is done on the original subject of these feelings. In all three examples, the transference feelings have been traced back to their original owner and the working through is done with regards to whoever the feelings were originally directed at, not the analyst. It is true that a psychoanalyst has to wait patiently for the transference trigger that will bring up the original memory to the fore. Hence, it is not the feelings that are directed towards the analyst on the basis of which causal inferences are made by the analyst; they are made on the basis of feelings experienced in reality by the patient and re-experienced in the session having been stirred up through the medium of the analyst. So, Grünbaum's objection that feelings directed towards the analyst, however similar to the original experience of P's childhood, cannot be the cause of P's symptom is true, but the objection is slightly misdirected.

Circular reasoning

The second objection of Grünbaum is that the reasoning from transference to the cause of symptom is circular. One needs to show independently that the childhood experiences were pathogenic for P.

Let us suppose that the correction of P's irrational attitudes towards the analyst leads to the resolution of the symptoms of P. For the sake of argument, I shall suppose that there are no rival explanations for the cure. Cure has been shown to be causally related to the correction of the general irrational tendencies that were manifested by P towards her analyst. If we grant that this is what is happening in an analytic situation, then we have a paradoxical situation. We have an attitude D and the resolution of D leads to the resolution of the symptoms of P, thus providing evidence that D is causally related to S. But D has a reverse temporal relation to S. D is a product of the analytic situation and should have no causal relation with the resolution of S, which is temporally antecedent to D. The only rational course to adopt is to accept the transference hypothesis; namely, that P's attitude towards the analyst has a much earlier origin. These are prototypes of conflicts she had originally directed towards her parents. They were merely transferred onto the analyst.

In fact, in the course of analysis, memories, incidents, conflicts and aggressive feelings towards such significant persons come up. And it is through their correction that the conflict is resolved. The attitude towards the analyst is the point of beginning. It gives the analyst an idea of what is going on in the mind of the patient regarding the significant persons in her life. Beginning from P's attitude towards him, he proceeds to bring up those memories and incidents and feelings of hostility that the patient actually harbours towards her father/parent. When the conflict is resolved and the patient has been able to develop enough ego strength to not feel threatened by her father, the symptoms disappear.

When an analyst makes a claim that by the resolution of the transference P has been cured of her symptoms, his claim is justified only if he can show that there is a causal relation between the resolution of the transference and the cure of the symptoms. (We must note that the transference resolution means that the relevant memories, thoughts, conflicts, etc. related to the original object have been brought up and resolved.) If this claim is justified, it indirectly supports the transference hypothesis; namely, that during the course of the treatment P tended to transfer her earlier emotional attitude onto the analyst. The transference hypothesis by itself does not make any causal claim. Its claim is limited merely to the transfer of emotions. The analyst can certainly accept the transference hypothesis tentatively, apply it for predicting certain events in the course of the treatment, and see whether the predictions come out true. This is not committing the fallacy of begging the question. It is an accepted strategy and by itself there is nothing logically fallacious about the process itself.

However, Grünbaum may have the following objections to my proposal: the transference hypothesis can never be justified without independent evidence that P did have the kind of earlier attitude towards her parents. Even if the attitude of P is bizarre towards the analyst, this is no evidence that her feelings are transference of her past. After all, P is in a bizarre situation—she is anxious; she is totally dependent on her therapist for the cure of her symptoms. Why should we not consider that her attitude is really the product of the analytic situation itself? There are two replies to this objection.

First, we are faced with a paradoxical situation if a cure is obtained by correcting the infantile attitude of transference. This is evidence that cure is causally related with the removal of an attitude that is temporally subsequent to the symptom. Thus the transference attitudes have to be hypothesised as being earlier in origin. Second, the analyst claims that nothing in the analytic situation warrants the kind of attitude that P develops towards her analyst. This is true of both positive and negative attitudes that P develops towards her analyst. As Freud pointed out in the case of the Rat Man:

> Things soon reached a point at which, in his dreams, his waking phantasies, and his associations, he began heaping the grossest and

> filthiest abuse upon me and my family, though in his deliberate actions, he never treated me with anything but the greatest respect. His demeanour as he repeated these insults to me was that of a man in despair. "How can a gentleman like you, sir," he used to ask, "let yourself be abused in this way by a low, good-for-nothing fellow like me? You ought to turn me out: that's all I deserve." (Freud, 1909b, p. 209)

This passage is quoted to point out that what P experiences in the analytic situation towards his analyst are, in most cases, completely unjustified by the situation itself. However, in the same case report Freud reports that the patient would get up from the couch and start roaming the room. The reason for this, as the patient himself explains, was that he wanted to put himself at a distance from Freud for fear that Freud might give him a beating. Freud reports that the patient recalled "that his father had had a passionate temper, and sometimes in his violence had not known where to stop" (Freud, 1909b, p. 209). Thus, through transference, the real memory of his father came up and the correction of these attitudes led to the removal of the symptoms.

I am assuming that the analyst is following the rules of analytic treatment; namely, he is neutral and does not have any personal relation to the patient. However, this by itself does not prove that the transference attitude could not be a product of the patient's relations with the doctor. But this fact, coupled with the cure brought about by the removal of the transference attitude, does provide strong support for the transference hypothesis.

Grünbaum may object that my entire argument rests on the causal relation between cure and the correction of attitude identified as pathogenic on the basis of transference. But in an analytic situation nothing can prove that the cure was due to the correction of these attitudes. To this, I reply by pointing out that I am merely making a conditional claim. I am merely stating under what conditions a claim based on transference is not logically fallacious. Whether such situations obtain in any given analytic situation is to be investigated. The analyst making the claim must point out that these conditions have been satisfied and the objector must show that these conditions have not been satisfied and that there is no evidence linking the correction of transference attitude to the cure of the symptoms.

In general, I agree with Grünbaum that many causal claims made by psychoanalysts are based on insufficient evidence, but this does not mean that the process is beyond correction. Part of the reason for this lax attitude of psychoanalysts is the emotional reality of the situation, which convinces them of the causal relation between different emotions and symptoms. This emotional reality is lost in any theoretical discussion. However, I do not disagree that appropriate evidence must be provided in substantiating a causal claim.

Section II

Experimental evidence

Finally, a few words about experimental evidence for psychoanalysis. After all, experimental evidence is considered to be the best of all evidence for any empirical enquiry. In *Foundations* Grünbaum merely mentions his conclusion regarding experimental evidence for psychoanalysis. He concludes that the evidence does not support any of the major psychoanalytic hypotheses. However, in the *BBS Symposium*, he gives a more detailed account of this evidence and reiterates his earlier conclusion. He says:

> Kline, Masling and Greenberg, however, point to a wealth of what they regard as important experimental "objective" or "quantitative" studies. Why, then, though I did cite Kline's (1981), Eysenck and Wilson's (1973), Fisher and Greenberg's (1977), Marmor's (1970), and Masling's (1983) work, did I not include any systematic discussion of this material in *Foundations*? And why did I claim that the extraclinical appraisal of Freud's "cardinal hypothesis … is largely a task of the future" (p. 278)?
>
> An evaluation on the basis of available studies would not have altered my conclusion about the empirical support for psychoanalysis, because the extraclinical data gathered so far, even when favourable, fail to support any of the major Freudian hypotheses whose clinical evidence I criticized as inadequate. (*BBS Symposium*, p. 269)

Grünbaum gives the following reasons for his conclusion: first, the results of major experimental studies at best establish the existence of certain types of psychological states that form part of some psychoanalytic hypotheses. For example, some studies provide evidence that there are repressed states; others that there are states of subliminal perception. They do not provide support for major psychoanalytic hypotheses that are essentially causal in nature; for example, repression is the cause of neuroses, repressed homosexuality is the cause of delusions, etc. Zamansky's (Fisher & Greenberg, 1978, p. 288–301) ingenious experiments on the correlation of homosexuality and paranoia and the experiments on subliminal perception belong to this category.

Second, Fisher and Greenberg have meticulously documented hundreds of experimental studies related to the validation of psychoanalytic hypotheses. Regarding their efforts, Grünbaum reiterates a comment made by Kline, "In our view, Fisher and Greenberg are quite uncritical ..." (*BBS Symposium*, p. 269). Third, a number of important studies need replication in order to prove the reliability of their results. The mammoth experiment done by Silverman ranging over a period of ten years belongs to this category.

And finally, favourable results of experimental studies on animals cannot be extrapolated directly and used to provide support to hypotheses concerning human beings. Experiments done on animals showing that conflicts can cause neurotic behaviours in animals; experiments on the effects of oral deprivation on the behaviour of animals, etc.; or Hoffman's prolonged study on the effect of maternal deprivation on monkeys belong to this category.

Therefore, Grünbaum concludes that sufficient experimental evidence in favour of major psychoanalytic hypotheses is yet to come. Accounts of prospective studies related to the testing of psychoanalytic hypotheses, if any, are included in the above account. It is not my intention to give a survey of all the experimental studies done to test psychoanalytic hypotheses and see whether they support Grünbaum's conclusions. I would like to make the following points: it is not clear what Grünbaum considers to be "support" for a hypothesis. Causal hypotheses are supported in different degrees. No causal hypotheses can be conclusively proved.

Grünbaum's summary rejection of innumerable experimental studies providing favourable evidence for psychoanalytic hypotheses makes one think whether he demands conclusive proof for a causal relation before being able to say that a particular causal hypothesis is "supported" by empirical evidence. I will readily grant Grünbaum the claim that no analytical causal hypothesis has conclusive experimental evidence in the sense mentioned above. But if "support" is taken in the sense of evidential support in different degrees, then there is sufficient support for many psychoanalytic hypotheses. There is sufficient evidence for anal character traits (see Fisher & Greenberg, 1978), some support for the relationship between anal eroticism and anal character traits (see Hilgard, Kubie, & Pumpian Mindlin, 2012, p. 16), quite a bit of support for the relationship between oral character traits and degree of oral satisfaction, etc. I am not claiming that any of this is conclusive, but neither is any hypothesis tested by Nisbett and Wilson or Prioleau, Murdock and Brody, whom Grünbaum is so fond of quoting. However, I would like to mention the following points in relation to Grünbaum's comments regarding experimental evidence for psychoanalysis.

Regarding Silverman's study, Grünbaum has quoted Erwin to make the point that there have been repeated failures to replicate Silverman's results. Furthermore, even if they were replicated, it does not prove that subliminal stimuli stir up unconscious fantasies. Lloyd Silverman's article, contradicts these reports. I quote:

> Subliminal psychodynamic activation experiments can be divided into two types: (a) laboratory studies of clinical and nonclinical populations in which experimental stimuli are intended to either intensify or reduce particular unconscious conflicts and thus exacerbate or diminish the degree of psychopathology manifested within a single laboratory session: and (b) therapy and "adjunct studies" in which clinical or non-clinical samples are assigned to either an experimental or control group, with each receiving subliminal stimulation over a period of time in an attempt to ascertain if the experimental stimulus can bring about more adaptive behaviour. *In over 60 studies*, the psychodynamic stimuli have produced effects that the control stimuli have not and in a way that has been consistent with psychoanalytic theory. (my emphasis) (Silverman, 1985, p. 249)

Are the favourable conclusions of these studies biased by the theoretical leanings of the experimenter? Silverman reports the following:

> What can be concluded from the research that has been cited in this article? In the words of one reviewer (Brody, 1980) whose background and activities eminently qualify him as a nonpartisan

> observer, the data from subliminal psychodynamic activation research offer "the strongest evidence for a psychoanalytic (i.e. dynamic) conception of the unconscious" (p. 280). In particular, the use of double-blind controls, the findings from the specificity studies (Hayden and Silverstein, 1982; Schmidt, 1982; Silverman, Bronstein, and Mendelsohn, 1978) and the replication in independent laboratories, would make it all but impossible to attribute the findings to artifactual influence. The non-psychoanalytic clinician may not want to address the "dynamic unconscious" in his clinical work but the results from this research (as well as findings from Reyher's laboratory made reference to earlier) make it clear, that such an unconscious was Freud's discovery, not his invention. (Silverman, 1985, p. 255)

Do these studies, in any way, support the causal hypothesis that the subliminal stimuli stir up unconscious fantasies? For one thing it is implied by the hypothesis that the contents of the subliminal stimuli stir up unconscious fantasies. This hypothesis would account for the difference in the intensification or the diminishment of the symptoms of the patients in the experimental group, provided rival hypotheses are ruled out. Silverman's article gives an account of three different studies done to rule out rival hypotheses.

> It might be of interest to know that Reyher and his colleagues have been working on hypnotic induction of neurotic conflict on laboratory subjects. False memories related to sexual and aggressive conflicts have been "implanted" in subjects under hypnotic states and emergence of neurotic symptoms consistent with psychoanalytic theory have been studied. (Silverman, 1985, p. 248)

Important studies are being conducted in hypnosis laboratories to test psychoanalytic hypotheses related to dreams and symbols. Some supporting evidence has emerged regarding symbolism in dreams.

Edward Erwin (1996) is quite critical of Silverman's marathon experiments. However, he is a little more cautious in his comments. He says:

> I think, it would be premature, then, to conclude that Silverman's experiments have corroborated certain Freudian hypotheses. Future results, of course, might yield a different verdict. It should

> also be noted that Silverman poses a problem for philosophers who claim, without qualification, that the psychoanalytic enterprise is pseudoscientific. He tried to obtain empirical evidence for psychoanalytic hypotheses through a long series of experiments and he made an honest effort to reply to many of his critics. (Erwin, 1996, pp. 208–209)

Also, Grünbaum cites Eysenck's criticism of Zamansky's experiment and considers it a cogent argument against any causal connection between latent homosexuality and paranoid delusion. In an ingeniously designed experiment Zamansky tested the latent homosexuality of the paranoids suffering from delusions. Both the control and the experimental groups were given pictures of various objects and asked to give an estimate of the surface area of different pictures. However, the real purpose of the study had nothing to do with the measurement of the area. It was hypothesised that the paranoids being latent homosexuals would look longer at the pictures of males than at the pictures of females. The hypothesis was supported by the results of the experiment.

There is no doubt that Eysenck's objection is an ad hoc one as pointed out by Kline. It is a commonly known observation that people do not look longer at something they are afraid of. It is well known that our natural tendency in case of fear is not to look at the object of fear but to avert one's gaze or to close one's eyes. Looking at a picture for a longer period of time because one is afraid of the object depicted in the picture is a hypothesis certainly not supported by common sense. This is not to say that Zamansky's experiment proves the hypothesis that latent homosexuality is the *cause* of paranoid delusion but it certainly is the first step in that direction. All quantitative studies in causal connection start by finding a strong correlation between the hypothesised cause and the effect. Once such a correlation is established, further studies can be done from other angles to provide support to the correlation. Thus, Zamansky's experiment does not directly support the causal connection between latent homosexuality and paranoid delusions, but given the improbability of such a connection, the findings make the hypothesis more plausible. The same is true of Lubrosky's (1974) groundbreaking study on momentary forgetting.

A similar argument can be applied to favourable results obtained from studies on animals. No one would argue that the results of studies done on animals can be directly extrapolated to human beings. Yet animal research has been one of the major sources of understanding the much more complicated human psychological and physical processes by providing the idea to test people in a more controlled environment. There are certain respects in which animals, particularly higher animals, are similar to human beings. Research done on intelligent animals cannot directly be extended to human beings, but it can render greater plausibility to such hypotheses. From this point of view Hoffman's classic experiment on the emotional impact of maternal deprivation makes it more plausible that human babies too may suffer from acute depression when deprived of their mother or mother-surrogate.

The Chicago Institute of Psychoanalysis conducted a carefully controlled inquiry to test the results of psychoanalytic therapy in follow-up studies. The studies resemble the closest approach to experimental testing and retesting of certain hypotheses in clinical situations. The results confirm some of the earlier hypotheses (see Schlessinger & Robbins, 1983).

I am not denying that a lot more research is needed for empirical validation of psychoanalytic theory and therapy. A good sign is that more and more work is being done in this area, thanks to Grünbaum's polemic against psychoanalysis. Some excellent work with strict scientific control has been done in the area of outcome studies. While the outcome of short-term psychoanalytical therapy is on par with cognitive behaviour therapy and/or interpersonal therapy, etc. the effect of long-term psychoanalytical therapy has been found to be consistently superior to other forms of therapy even after as long an interval as 6.7 years. (See Leuzinger-Bohleber et al., 2002; Sandell et al., 1999; Knekt et al., 2008; Marttunen et al., 2008; Leichsenring & Rabung, 2008, pp. 1551–1565; Shedler, 2010). The International Psychoanalytical Association has published the second edition of outcome studies (2001) under the able editorship of Peter Fonagy. The results are highly encouraging and provide hope for the future but psychoanalysts cannot afford to remain complacent. I end with Peter Fonagy's cautionary advice:

> Psychoanalysis needs to change. Gathering further evidence for psychoanalysis through outcome studies is important, not simply to improve support for existing practices, but far more to generate a change of attitude in psychoanalytic practitioners. This is essential to ensure a future for psychoanalysis and psychoanalytic therapies. (Fonagy, 2000, pp. 620–623)

FURTHER READING

Achinstein (Ed.) (1983). *The Concept of Evidence*. New York: Oxford University Press.

Adair, J. G., & Spinner, B. (1981). Subjects' access to cognitive process: Demand characteristic and verbal report. *Journal of Theory and Social Behavior, 11, 1*: 31–52.

Bellak, L., & Smith, M. B. (1956). An experimental exploration of the psychoanalytic process. *The Psychoanalytic Quarterly, 25*: 385–414.

Berger, L. S. (1993). Review of Adolf Grünbaum's validation in the clinical theory of psychoanalysis: A study in the philosophy of psychoanalysis, *Psychological Issues, 22*: 462–470.

Berrigan, L. P., Kurtz, R. M., Stabile, J. P., & Strube, M. J. (1991). Durability of "posthypnotic suggestions" as a function of type of suggestion and trance depth. *The International Journal of Clinical and Experimental Hypnosis, 34, 1*: 24–38.

Brenner, C. (1955). *An Elementary Text Book of Psychoanalysis*. New York: International University Press.

Burke, T. E. (1983). *The Philosophy of Popper*. Manchester University Press.

Earman, J. (Ed.) (1983). *Testing Scientific Theories. Minnesota Studies in the Philosophy of Science, 10*. Minneapolis, MN: University of Minnesota Press.

Enrico, E. J., Cumming, J. D., & Horowitz, M. J. (1988). Another look at the non-specific hypothesis of therapeutic effectiveness. *Journal of Consulting and Clinical Psychology, 56, 1*: 48–55.

Erwin, E. (1980). Psychoanalysis: How firm is the evidence? *Nous, 14, 3*: 443–456.

Erwin, E. (1993). Philosophers on Freudianism: In: J. Earman, Janis, A. Massey, G., & Rescher, N. (Eds.), *Philosophical Problems of the Internal and External World, Festschrift in Honor of Adolf Grünbaum* (pp. 409–460). Pittsburgh University Press.

Fromm, E., & Brown, D. (1986). *Hypnotherapy and Hypnoanalysis*. Lawrence Erlbaum Associates: Mahwah, NJ.

Giere, R. (1984). *Understanding Scientific Reasoning*. New York: Holt, Rinehart and Wilson.

Glymour, C. (1980). *Theory and Evidence*. Princeton University Press.

Goldman, R. N. & Weinberg, J. S. (1985). *Statistics: An Introduction*. Princeton, NJ: Prentice-Hall.

Gomez, L. (2005). *The Freud Wars: An Introduction to the Philosophy of Psychoanalysis*. New York: Routledge.

Grünbaum, A. (1976). Is the method of bold conjecture and attempted refutations justifiably the method of science? *British Journal for the Philosophy of Science, 27*, 2: 105–136.

Grünbaum, A. (1976). Ad hoc auxiliary hypotheses and falsificationism. *British Journal for the Philosophy of Science, 27, 4*: 329–362.

Grünbaum, A. (1986). The placebo concept in medicine and psychiatry. *Psychological Medicine, England, 16, 1*: 19–38.

Harding, S. (Ed.) (1976). *Can Theories be Refuted? Essays on the Duhem-Quine Thesis*. Boston, MA: D. Reidel.

Hempel, C. G. (1965). *Aspects of Scientific Explanation and Other Essays in the Philosophy of Science*. New York: Free Press.

Hilgard, E. R. (1965). *Hypnotic Susceptibility*. New York: Harcourt Brace and World Press.

Klingemann, H. K. H. (1992). Coping and maintenance strategies of spontaneous remitters from problem use of alcohol and heroin in Switzerland. *International Journal of the Addictions, 27, 12*: 1359–1388.

Kyburg, H. E. Jr. (1984). *Theory and Measurement*. New York: Cambridge University Press.

Kyburg, H. E. Jr. (1988). Cognition and causality. In: S. Schiffer & Steele, S. (Eds.), *Cognition and Representation* (pp. 21–33). Boulder, CO: Westview.

Luborsky, L. et al. (1985). Verification of Freud's grandest clinical hypothesis: The transference. *Clinical Psychological Review, 5*: 231–246.

Lynn, S. J., Neufeld, V., & Maré, C. (1993). Direct vs. indirect suggestion: A conceptual and methodological review. *The International Journal of Clinical and Experimental Hypnosis, XLI, 2*: 124–152.

Lyons, W. (1985). The behaviouristic struggle with introspection. *International Philosophical Quarterly, 25*: 139–156.

Mayman, M. (Ed.) (1973). *Psychoanalytic Research: Three Approaches to the Experimental Study of Subliminal Process*. New York: International Universities Press.

Musgrave, A. (1975). Popper's diminishing returns from repeated tests. *Australian Journal of Philosophy, 53, 3*: 248–253.

Parloff, M. B. (1984). Psychotherapy research and its incredible credibility crisis. *Medical Psychology Review, 4*: 95–109.

Pierre, D. (1954). *The Aim and Structure of Physical Theory*. Princeton University Press.

Rakover, S. (1983). Hypothesizing from introspection: A model for the role of entities in psychological explanations. *Journal of Theory of Social Behavior, 13, 2*: 211–230.

Rapaport, D., & Gill, M. M. (1959). The points of view and assumptions of metapsychology. *International Journal of Psychoanalysis, 40*: 153–162.

Silverman, L. H. (1977). Psychoanalytic theory: The reports of my death are greatly exaggerated. In: R. Stern, Horowitz, L. S., & Lyons, T. (Eds.), *Science and Psychotherapy* (pp. 255–282). New York: Haven Publishing.

Simkins, L. (1982). Biofeed: Clinically valid or oversold? *Psychological Record, 32*: 3–7.

Towney, J. W. (1983). *Single Subject Research in Special Education*. Columbus, OH: Merrill.

Waterhouse, G. J. & Strupp, H. H. (1984). The patient-therapist relationship: Research from the psychodynamic perspective. *Social Psychology Review, 4*: 77–92.

REFERENCES

Barber, T. X., & Calverley, D. X. (1964). An experimental study of "hypnotic" (auditory and visual) hallucinations. *Journal of Abnormal and Social Psychology, 68*: 13–20.

Bellak, L. (1971). Editorial. *Journal of the Nervous and Mental Diseases, 165*: 5.

Bergin, A. E. (1971). The evaluation of therapeutic outcomes. In: A. E. Bergin & Garfield, S. L. (Eds.), *Handbook on Psychotherapy and Behaviour Change: An Empirical Analysis* (pp. 217–270). New York: Wiley.

Bowers, K. S. (1967). The effects of demand for honesty on reports of visual and auditory hallucinations. *International Journal for Clinical and Experimental Hypnosis, 15, 3*: 31–36.

Bowers, K. S. (1976). *Hypnosis for the Seriously Curious.* Monterey, CA: Brooks/Cole.

Cioffi, F. (1985). Psychoanalysis, pseudo-science and testability in Popper and the human sciences. In: C. Gregory & Musgrave, A. (Eds.), (pp. 13–44). Boston: Kluwer Academic.

Eagle, M. (1985). The current status of psychoanalysis. *Clinical Psychological Review, 5*: 259–269.

Edelson, M. (1985). *Hypothesis and Evidence in Psychoanalysis.* University of Chicago Press.

Erdelyi, M. H. (1985). *Psychoanalysis Freud's Cognitive Psychology.* New York: Freeman.

Erwin, E. (1996). *A Final Accounting: Philosophical and Empirical Issues in Freudian Psychology*. Cambridge, MA: MIT Press.

Eysenck, H. J. (1952). The effect of psychotherapy: An evaluation. *Journal of Consulting Psychology, 16*: 319–324.

Fenichel, O. (1945). *Problems of Psychoanalytic Technique*. New York: Psychoanalytic Quarterly.

Fisher, S., & Greenberg, R. P. (Eds.), (1978). *The Scientific Evaluation of Freud's Theory and Therapy: A Book of Readings*. New York: Basic Books.

Fonagy, P. (2000). The outcome of psychoanalysis: The hope of a future. *The Psychologist, 13, 12*: 620–623.

Freud, S., & Breuer, J. (1895d). *Studies on Hysteria. S. E., 2*. London: Hogarth.

Freud, S. (1896a). Heredity and the etiology of neuroses. *S. E., 3*: 147, 21, 23, 125–126, 134–135, 143–156, 163, 191, 255, 271. London: Hogarth.

Freud, S. (1905a). On psychotherapy. *S. E., 7*: 257–268, 283–301. London: Hogarth.

Freud, S. (1908d). "Civilized" sexual morality and modern nervous illness. *S. E., 9*: 186. London: Hogarth.

Freud, S. (1909b). Analysis of a phobia in a five-year-old boy. *S. E., 10*: 3–147. London: Hogarth.

Freud, S. (1916–1917). Transference. *S. E., 16*: 431–447. London: Hogarth.

Freud, S. (1916–1917). Analytic therapy. *S. E., 16*: 448–463. London: Hogarth.

Freud, S. (1918b). From the history of an infantile neurosis. *S. E., 17*: 3–123. London: Hogarth.

Freud, S. (1919a). Lines of advance in psychoanalytic therapy. *S. E., 17*: 158–168. London: Hogarth.

Freud, S. (1925d). *An Autobiographical Study. S. E., 20*: 27. London: Hogarth.

Freud, S. (1926d). *Inhibition, symptoms, and anxiety. S. E., 20*: 179–258. London: Hogarth.

Freud, S. (1933a). Explanations, applications and orientations. *S. E., 22*: 136–157. London: Hogarth.

Fromm, E., & Shore, R. (1979). *Hypnosis: Development in Research and New Perspective*. New York: Aldine.

Greenson, R. (1967). *The Technique and Practice of Psychoanalysis*. London: Hogarth.

Grünbaum, A. (1977). How scientific is psychoanalysis? In: R. Stern, Horowitz, L. S. & Lyons, T. (Eds.), *Science and Psychotherapy* (pp. 219–254). New York: Haven.

Grünbaum, A. (1979). Is Freudian psychoanalytic theory pseudo-Scientific by Karl Popper's criterion of demarcation? *American Philosophical Quarterly, 16, 2*: 131–141.

Grünbaum, A. (1984). *Foundations of Psychoanalysis: A Philosophical Critique.* Oakland, CA: University of California Press.

Grünbaum, A. (1986). Précis of the foundations of psychoanalysis: A philosophical critique. *Behavioral and Brain Sciences, 9, 2*: 217–284.

Grünbaum, A. (1988). The role of case-study method in the foundations of psychoanalysis. *Canadian Journal of Philosophy, 18, 4*: 623–658.

Grünbaum, A. (1993). *Validation in the Clinical Theory of Psychoanalysis.* Madison, CT: International University Press.

Hilgard, E. R., Kubie, L. S., & Pumpian-Mindlin, E. (2012). *Psychoanalysis as Science: The Hixon Lectures on the Scientific Status of Psychoanalysis.* Whitefish, MT: Literary Licensing, LLC.

Hirschmüller, A. (1989). *The Life and Work of Josef Breuer.* New York University Press.

Hook, S. (1964). *Psychoanalysis, Scientific Method and Philosophy.* New York University Press.

Knekt et al. (2008). Randomized trial on the effectiveness of long-and short-term psychodynamic psychotherapy and solution focussed therapy on psychiatric symptoms during a three-year follow-up. *Psychological Medicine, 38, 5*: 689–703.

Kradin, R. (2008). *The Placebo Response and the Power of Unconscious Healing.* New York: Routledge.

Kyburg, H. E. Jr. (1990). *Science and Reason.* New York: Oxford University Press.

Leichsenring, F., & Rabung, S. (2008). Effectiveness of long-term psychodynamic psychotherapy: A meta-analysis. *The Journal of American Medical Association, 300*: 1551–1565.

Leuzinger-Bohleber, M. (2002). The psychoanalytic follow-up study (DPV: A representative naturalistic study of psychoanalyses and psychoanalytic long-term therapies). In: M. Leuzinger-Bohleber & Target, M. (Eds.), *The Outcomes of Psychoanalytic Treatment.* London: Whurr.

Lillienfeld, A. M. (1976). *Foundations of Epidemiology.* New York, Oxford University Press.

Lilienfeld, A. M., & Lilienfeld, D. E. (1980). *Foundations of Epidemiology.* New York: Oxford University Press.

Luborsky, L., & Mintz, J. (1974). What sets off momentary forgetting during a psychoanalysis? *Psychoanalysis and Contemporary Science, 5*: 231–246.

Lynn, S. J., Neufeld, V., & Matyi, C. L. (1987). Inductions vs. suggestions: Effects of direct and indirect wording on hypnotic responding and experience. *Journal of Abnormal Psychology, 96, 1*: 76–79.

Marttunen, M., Valikoki, M., Lindfors, O., & Lakaasonen, M. A., et al. (2008). Pretreatment clinical and psychosocial predictors of remission from depression after short-term psychodynamic psychotherapy and solution focused psychotherapy: A 1-year follow-up study. *Psychotherapy Research, 18,* 2: 191–199.

McNeilly, C. L., & Howard, K. (1991). The effect of psychotherapy: A reevaluation based on dosage. *Psychotherapy Research, 1, 1*: 74–78.

Meehl, P. E. (1983). Subjectivity in psychoanalytic inference: The nagging persistence of Wilhelm Fliess's Achensee question. In: J. Earman (Ed.), *Testing Scientific Theories, X* (pp. 315–412). Minneapolis, MN: University of Minnesota Press.

Mill, J. S. (1950). *Philosophy of Scientific Method, edited with an introduction by Earnest Nagel*. New York: Hafner.

Nisbett, R. E., & Wilson, T. D. (1977). Telling more than we can know: Verbal report on mental processes. *Psychological Review, 84, 3*: 231–259.

Pap, A. (1962). *An Introduction to the Philosophy of Science*. New York: The Free Press of Glencoe.

Popper, K. (1959). *The Logic of Scientific Discovery*. New York: Harper Torchbooks, 1968.

Popper, K. (1963). *Conjectures and Refutations: The Growth of Scientific Knowledge*. New York: Harper Torchbooks, 1968.

Prioleau, L., Murdock, M., & Brody, N. (1983). An analysis of psychotherapy vs. placebo. *Behavioral and Brain Sciences, 6*: 275–285.

Rimm, D. C., & Masters, J. C. (1979). *Behavior Therapy: Techniques and Empirical Findings*. New York: Academic Press.

Rothman, K. (1986). *Modern Epidemiology*. Boston, MA: Little Brown.

Rubinstein, B. B. (1980). On the psychoanalytic theory of unconscious motivation and the problem of its confirmation. *Nous, 14, 3*: 427–442.

Salmon, W. (1971). *Statistical Explanation and Statistical Relevance*. University of Pittsburgh Press.

Sandell et al. (1999). Long-term findings of Stockholm outcome of psychoanalysis and psychotherapy project, presented at the meeting of Psychoanalytic Long-term Treatments: A Challenge for Clinical and Empirical Research in Psychoanalysis, Hamburg.

Schlessinger, N., & Robbin, F. P. (1983). *A Developmental View of the Psychoanalytic Process*. Madison, CT: International Universities Press.

Schweitzer, J. (1984). What happens in spontaneous remission of neuroses? A study of four cases. *Nervenarzt, 55, 5*: 249–256.

Shedler, J. (2010). The efficacy of psychodynamic psychotherapy. *American psychologist, 65,* 2: 98–109.

Silverman, L. H. (1985). Research on psychoanalytic psychodynamic proposition. *Clinical Psychological Review, 5*: 247–257.

Skyrms, B. (1966). *Choice and Chance: An Introduction to Inductive Logic*. Encino, CA: Dickenson.

Smith, E. R., & Miller, F. D. (1978). Limits on the perception of the cognitive processes: A reply to Nisbett and Wilson. *Psychological Review, 85, 4*: 355–362.

Spanos, N. P., & Barber, T. X. (1968). "Hypnotic" experiences as inferred from auditory and visual hallucinations. *Journal of Experimental Research in Personality, 3*: 136–150.

Stone, J. A. (1985). Behaviour compliance with direct and indirect body movement suggestions. *Journal of Abnormal Psychology, 94, 3*: 256–263.

Wagstaff, G. F. (1981). Hypnosis, Compliance and Belief. Sussex: Harvester.

Wollheim, R. (Ed.), (1977). *Philosophers on Freud*. New York: J. Aronson, 1982.

INDEX

For Product Safety Concerns and Information please contact our EU representative GPSR@taylorandfrancis.com
Taylor & Francis Verlag GmbH, Kaufingerstraße 24, 80331 München, Germany

www.ingramcontent.com/pod-product-compliance
Lightning Source LLC
Chambersburg PA
CBHW070327270326
41926CB00017B/3795

* 9 7 8 1 7 8 2 2 0 4 0 6 0 *